COMPARATIVE LAW AND SOCIAL THEORY

Previously Published
in the Edward Douglass White Lecture Series

Robert M. Hutchins, Education for Freedom

Edward S. Corwin, Liberty Against Government

Paul H. Appleby, Morality and Administration in Democratic Government

Leonard D. White, States and the Nation

Jefferson B. Fordham, A Larger Concept of Community

Walter Gellhorn, Individual Freedom and Governmental Restraints

A. T. Mason, The Supreme Court from Taft to Warren

Robert J. Harris, The Quest for Equality: The Constitution, Congress and the Supreme Court

Arthur Larson, When Nations Disagree

Frederick L. Schuman, The Cold War: Retrospect and Prospect

COMPARATIVE LAW
and SOCIAL THEORY

JEROME HALL

Louisiana State University Press
1963

Copyright 1963 by
Louisiana State University Press

Library of Congress Catalog Card Number: 63-20406

Manufactured in the United States of America by
Vail-Ballou Press, Inc., Binghamton, New York

Designed by Gary Gore

FOREWORD

The invitation to give the 1962 Edward Douglass White Lectures at Louisiana State University provided an opportunity to apply theories of long-standing interest to very important problems. The lectures, given in April, 1962, have been completely rewritten and incorporated into various parts of this book.

Twenty-five years ago the work of Dean Paul M. Hebert and other colleagues at Louisiana State University aroused my interest in comparative law, and it was as the representative of this law faculty that I attended the Hague meeting of the International Society of Comparative Law in 1937. Since those early years I have had many occasions to further my study of the common law of crimes by comparing it with European criminal law.

The thesis of this book is the outgrowth of that experience and an interest in philosophy and social science which began more than forty years ago when I was a student at the University of Chicago; and my indebtedness to Frank H. Knight, George H. Mead, Charles E. Merriam and Albion W. Small will be apparent even though I have departed in various ways from the teaching of these scholars, due, perhaps, to my specialization in law. The thesis of this book did not take definite form until I lectured on comparative law and legal sociology and conferred with scholars in Mexico and South America in 1960, and gave seminars in legal philosophy and criminal law at the University of Freiburg, Germany, in 1961. An additional opportunity to formulate my views on the subject of this book was provided in August of that year in the preparation of several lectures on the philosophy of comparative law given at the International Faculty of Comparative Law in Luxembourg.

v

Fortunately, the invitation to give the White Lectures arrived when I was in Europe on sabbatical leave of absence from Indiana University, and a grant by The Rockefeller Foundation made it possible to continue my work there on these problems for several additional months. I wish to thank Mr. K. Howard Drake and his staff, who made available the excellent facilities of the Institute of Advanced Legal Studies, London, and Sous-Directeur Yvonne Marx and her associates, who gave me generous assistance at the Centre Français de Droit Comparé, Paris.

The hospitality of my old friends and colleagues during the days of the lectureship in Baton Rouge lingers in my memory and will not soon be forgotten.

JEROME HALL

Bloomington, Indiana
May 30, 1963

CONTENTS

COMPARATIVE LAW AND SOCIAL THEORY

1

THEORIES OF
COMPARATIVE LAW

The differences among human beings often dissolve in the discovery of their basic similarities and, in any case, they become intelligible when viewed in the context of a known pattern. Limited as we are, we begin with self-knowledge and self-love, and when we discover ourselves in ever-widening dimensions of common experience, friendship and affection increase. This is the underlying emotional basis of comparative study in law and social science, which adds momentum to the scholar's quest for truth. Thus, the world-wide social and political changes and the attendant "mingling of cultures" which mark this century have greatly accelerated interest in comparative study.

Comparison is, of course, as old as our most primitive ancestors; and the preliterate geniuses who invented the wheel and the bow and arrow had natural models to guide the construction of their artifacts. Quite different, however, is appreciation of "the comparative method" to the extent of making it the principal point of emphasis in many social disciplines. That is a nineteenth-century phenomenon—the direct result of the revolutionary progress of philology and biology.

In 1786 Sir William Jones, a judge in the High Court at Calcutta, pointed out the "strong affinity" between Sanskrit, Greek, Latin, and several modern languages, and he suggested that they all "have sprung from some common source." [1] His discovery did not bear fruit until thirty years later, when the first contributions of Franz Bopp and Rasmus Rask were published. Grimm's *German Grammar* followed in 1819–1822, and in 1833 Bopp brought

3

out his *Comparative Grammar.* When William Dwight Whitney, Professor of Sanskrit and Comparative Philology in Yale College, wrote *The Life and Growth of Language* (1875), it was evident that a new science had been born—the direct product of the comparative study of linguistic forms.[2]

Even more far-reaching in its effects was the impact of nineteenth-century biology.[3] Cuvier's *Leçons d'Anatomie Comparée* (1801–1805) and, in the United States, the work of E. D. Cope placed comparative anatomy on a firm basis. Histology, physiology, and bacteriology (Pasteur, 1822–1895) became established sciences, and in all of them comparison was prominent. It was in organic evolution, however, that the most dramatic discoveries were made. The publication in 1735 of Linnaeus' classification gave Cuvier a definite plan which he improved in ways that had much greater scientific significance. By the time Lamarck (1774–1829) was making his basic contributions, including his theory of evolution, biological classification had made available considerable knowledge of definite types of organisms, facilitating the further progress of the science. Almost every page of Darwin's *Origin of Species* (1859) and *Descent of Man* (1871), for example, includes comparisons of the structure, functions, and traits of many animals;[4] the importance of "the comparative method" was obvious. The rise of comparative philology, comparative anatomy, comparative sociology, comparative law, comparative politics, comparative religion, and other "comparative" disciplines in the nineteenth century reflected the pervasive influence of the achievements of comparative study. Intrigued by many cultures from which the data of our studies are increasingly gathered, we, too, are held in the spell of "the comparative method," while the inordinate pressures of our times emphasize the necessity of improving the relevant disciplines in order to acquire the desired knowledge.

One could begin his intellectual adventure at any one of the above indicated points, for the paths marked out by the scholars who cultivated those disciplines eventually converge. But there are very good reasons for emphasizing comparative law. Comparative law was from its beginning closely associated with linguistics, anthropology, history, politics, and sociology; theorizing about comparative law has been especially challenging. The questions raised are equally significant for the other disciplines.

Presumably, comparative legal research implies that there is important knowledge to be acquired which cannot be had in any other way. In many quarters this is a mere truism but there is a widely held theory which seems to reject this assumption, and there is also a very critical view of comparative law: "The greatest confusion continues to prevail . . . The consequence is a literature that is voluminous, obsessively repetitious, and sterile. . . ."[5] Very different questions are involved in these estimates of comparative law, as we shall see. But it may be suggested immediately that it is the incongruity between the value of many comparative legal studies and the disagreement regarding elementary questions about "comparative law" which raise important problems.

If one takes a critical look at the extant literature of comparative law, it is not difficult to discover many limitations in it as well as many puzzles. Much of it seems to be addressed only to other experts. Some of it recalls the arid conceptualism which troubled Jhering and many of his successors, despite avowals of the importance of the "social context" and the "function" of laws. One reason for the omission of discussion on these cultural matters is the fact that, unlike the reports of anthropologists on primitive law, most comparative legal studies have been written on modern law by Western legal scholars for Western-educated legal readers; hence the result is often of parochial significance rather than an important increase in knowledge. Many comparative studies have practical purposes, and these augment the diversity of the voluminous publications entitled "comparative law." A substantial literature on foreign law does not include anything more than casual references to similar laws or legal institutions, yet it is often classified as "comparative law." Even scholarly participants in the comparative enterprise (I have in mind an eminent European professor of comparative law) believe that so-called "comparative law" is only a serial discussion of the laws of two or more countries set down in the physical juxtaposition of printed words.

Whatever else these estimates imply, they indicate that comparative law—if it exists in any defensible sense—is in an extremely problematical, if not precarious, condition. The fact seems to be that the comparatist must rely almost entirely upon his individual judgment in deciding which criteria are significant, how to go about his work, and what sort of contribution he should try to make. In these circumstances, it would require rare courage to undertake to prove that everything called "comparative law" makes any definite kind of sense or that everything written even by the soundest comparatists constitutes a unified body of knowledge.

On the other hand, it is obvious that some comparative legal studies make very good sense, and it ought to be possible to discover their basic features. There is also the personal experience of learning a great deal in the process of comparing a branch of one's national law with that of a foreign system. It is equally certain that one acquires considerable knowledge in reading comparative studies for which he is prepared. These experiences definitely indicate that there is some kind of knowledge in comparative law and, presumably, it would be very desirable to discover its characteristics.

The diverse estimates noted above reflect various theories of comparative law, not merely different uses of those words. It is possible, and it might be significant, to determine the dozen or more meanings that have been given "comparative law." But this would not solve the problems that trouble comparatists. They know that "comparative law" is employed in various senses; and it would be only a restatement of their problems to say that they are concerned with the best use of the term. "Best" obviously depends upon purpose, and scholars are truth-seekers, whatever else may motivate their work. We are accordingly required to ask some difficult questions about comparative law. We must take account of the publications of comparatists, what they say ought to be done to improve comparative scholarship, and, especially, of theories of comparative law. All of this presupposes the existence of comparative law in some form or degree. Accordingly, what one can derive from the extant published studies, the present work of legal comparatists, and the future course of comparative scholarship are all dependent for one reason or another upon whether a sound answer can be given the elementary question—what is comparative law? The first step towards a defensible answer is to recognize that this is not a question in the field of comparative law. It is not a problem in the solution of which all comparatists may be expected to have special competence.[6] It is, instead, a jurisprudential problem. By like token, sweeping statements by legal philosophers (for example, that the main difference between Continental law and common law is that the method of the former is deductive while that of the latter is inductive) may not be significant by reference to canons of comparative scholarship.[7] It is true, of course, that some scholars are both comparatists and legal philosophers. But—in the present state of comparative law, at least— we cannot obtain an easy answer to the question "What is comparative law?" by consulting comparatists. For, just as most physicists would make a poor showing if called upon to discuss the philosophy of physics, so one should not be surprised if even distinguished legal comparatists were not always persuasive when they discussed the nature of comparative law—despite the fact that their observations on that subject may be very suggestive.

If, with the above caveat in mind, we view the current scene and indulge in some simplification, to be corrected later, we find many legal comparatists arrayed in two camps, one espousing the banner of Method, the other, that of Social Science.

A Method

The gist of the former position is that, despite the connotation of the English words, comparative law is a method—"the method of comparison." This thesis was presented by Frederick Pollock at the first International Congress of Comparative Law, held in Paris in 1900, where he said, "Le droit comparé n'est pas une science propre, mais qu'il n'est que l'introduction de la méthode comparée dans le droit." [8] This view of comparative law was discussed by De Francisci,[9] but it was elaborated and given such wide currency by the late Professor H. C. Gutteridge that it has come to be attributed to him. It was adopted by Professor C. J. Hamson, his successor in the Chair of Comparative Law at Cambridge University, by Professor René David of the University of Paris, who had also been a student of Gutteridge, and by many other scholars.[10]

When Gutteridge said, " 'Comparative Law' denotes a method of study and research," he added, "and not a distinct branch or department of the law. If by 'law' we mean a body of rules," he continued, "it is obvious that there can be no such thing as 'comparative' law . . . [i.e.] any independent rules for the regulation of human relationships or transactions." [11] If the thesis that comparative law is a method of study had been limited to what was suggested in the above context, no problem might have arisen, for it seems plain that there is no comparative positive law in the literal sense in which contract law and criminal law are branches of national legal systems. A question might be raised, to be sure, regarding the place of the elucidation of common legal concepts in national legal theory; that is, do not comparatists contribute to the knowledge of national law? [12] But propositions stating the resemblances found among certain laws are obviously not positive laws.

Gutteridge, however, went far beyond the context of the above observations, saying, ". . . the subject-matter [of comparative law], being non-existent, is one which defies definition"; and ". . . comparative law is merely a convenient label attached to a particular method of study and research." [13] In sum, his theory is that comparative law is *only* a method. At first sight this is a rather startling position, especially when maintained by a distinguished comparatist. No one, apparently, has maintained that comparative philology or comparative politics or comparative anatomy is *only* the method of comparison. But it might be argued that the prevailing assumption regarding these disciplines only reflects the lack of critical appraisal of those subjects.

That Gutteridge's theory has sweeping implications is evident since comparison is not in the least peculiar to law or to any legal discipline. Every scientist uses the method of comparison; and if comparative law is only the method of comparison, there is nothing to distinguish it from physics, biology, or any other science or social discipline except in terms of "substantive" characteristics which these bodies of knowledge have, but which comparative law lacks. Indeed, comparison is also the method of the man in the street, employed constantly and, evidently, every time he makes one decision rather than another. To be *sapiens* is to be a comparatist. As the Scandinavian philosopher, Harald Höffding, put it: "To think is to compare—to find difference and similarity." [14] But, it must be immediately added, it would fall far short of justice or accuracy to suggest that Gutteridge's theory can be dismissed on the ground that its only characterization of comparative law is that it is like scientific method and everyday thought. To understand the significance of his theory, one must place it in the context of the history of comparative law and vis à vis current competing theories. This we shall shortly do.

We must also avoid exaggerating the actual differences among these comparatists; it is well, therefore, to call attention to certain other views held by those whom we may, for convenience, call the methodologists. For example, Gutteridge acknowledged that "Montesquieu, in particular, has a claim to be considered as the founder of comparative law." It is worth adding (since Montesquieu is also widely regarded as the founder of the sociology of law) that Gutteridge lauded his work because it was he "who first realized that a rule of law should not be treated as an abstraction, but must be regarded against a background of its history and of the environment in which it is called upon to function." [15] Gutteridge even said: "The laws must be examined in the light of their political, social or economic purpose, and regard must be paid to their dynamic rather than to their static or doctrinal aspects." He also recognized, rather hesitantly, the validity of a classification of comparative law into Descriptive Comparative Law, which merely furnishes information, and Applied Comparative Law, which may be purely theoretical; and the connotations of both are substantive, not merely methodological, ones.[16]

So, too, Professor Hamson speaks of the comparative method as an aid to understanding law "in its function as a social institution in our society." [17] Going beyond these hints is the discussion of Professor David who, while he also avows that comparative law is only a method, states that the knowledge of society and of practically the whole of culture is essential in comparative study.[18] It is important to bear in mind, therefore, that the methodologists' view of comparative law includes references to the social context, the social institution, and the function of laws, even if a question immediately arises as to the consistency of these references with the theory that comparative law is only a method.

Sociology of Law

What is only a suggestion among the methodologists comprises a definite theory of comparative law, which also attracts wide adherence among legal scholars. The gist of this theory is that comparative law is a type of knowledge, a social science. In France this theory of comparative law was formulated by Saleilles, Lambert, and Lévy-Ullmann; in Germany the work of Kohler, Rabel, and others is closely related to this view of comparative law.[19] Lambert, a student of Saleilles, was among the first to recognize the social scientific intent of comparative law.[20] Rabel also emphasized the study of the "social purpose of the rules and the service of the concepts to this purpose . . . aptly called the functional approach," and he included ethnological jurisprudence and historical comparison in the field of comparative law.[21] Among contemporary European scholars, Professor Brutau closely associates comparative law with the sociology of law.[22]

In the United States, although Kent and Story made use of foreign treatises in reaching their decisions, professional comparative law may be said to have begun with Wigmore's publication in 1897 of "The Pledge-Idea: A Study of Comparative Legal Ideas." The influence of biology and Maine is evident in his analysis of the development of the pledge-idea in accordance with the evolution of economic change and in his conclusion that "the progress has been from a primitive forfeit-idea to a later collateral-security idea."[23]

Thirty-four years later Wigmore discussed his study in an illuminating bit of self-analysis that revealed the sociological trend in comparative law in the United States. He was still primarily interested in the evolution of legal ideas and he hailed Maine as "a true apostle of comparative law."[24] Yet, he wrote: "But in my [1897] exposition no account was taken of the differing economic, social, religious or other conditions of the various peoples and countries which could explain the variations found in their respective laws. Merely the legal rules were traced. Thus the account was not, in any full sense, an explanation of the evolution of the idea . . . Today such a mode of exposition would never be regarded as final. It forms only the skeleton of a treatment of legal evolution." [25] In 1931 Wigmore emphasized the "background of the social and ethical and economic facts and ideas in which the system of law thrives at a particular period." [26]

By that time Pound had made sociological jurisprudence well known in the United States. In 1917 he said, "[T]he most significant movement in modern legal science is the rise of the functional point of view. . . ." Later, Pound referred to a "functional comparison" which, for him, meant "the working of legal precepts" and "how and how far they attain their ends and the ends of law in the time and place." [27] He also referred to "a functional standpoint" in the "comparison of technique, comparison of received ideal, comparison of doctrines and conceptions and modes of developing grounds of decision on the basis of the authoritative legal materials. . . ." [28] But he did not make any detailed application of sociological jurisprudence to the problems of comparative law.

In 1938 Professor Max Rheinstein, influenced by Rabel and finding the sociological habit of American legal thought similarly disposed, excluded the mere description of foreign laws from the field; he wrote that the term comparative law "should be reserved to denominate those kinds of scientific treatment of law which go beyond the taxonomic or analytical description or technical application of one or more systems of positive law." This scientific treatment he found in two areas—the functional comparison of rules of law and "the social function of law in general." "In this sense," he stated, "comparative law is synonymous with Sociology of Law." Concluding, however, that a sociology of law "hardly exists," he would for the present confine instruction to the "functional comparison of legal rules and institutions." [29] Returning to the subject fifteen years later in a more optimistic mood, Professor Rheinstein wrote that comparative law "is the observational and exactitude-seeking science of law in general . . . it searches for . . . laws in the sense in which the word is used in the 'sciences,' laws of the kind of Newton's laws of gravitation . . . laws . . . in that sense in which the word is understood in modern natural science. . . ." He added that he was using the term "comparative law in the sense of sociology of law."[30] In a similar vein Professor Yntema, who, in addition, emphasized a humanistic approach, said, "Comparative law is another name for legal science. . . ."[31]

The Issues Joined

Some pertinent questions must be raised about the alleged synonymity of comparative law and legal sociology or legal science, as defined above. There is, first, the question: If comparative law is only another name for legal sociology or legal science, why use it at all? Indeed, that usage seems to support the thesis of methodologists who argue that the knowledge acquired by comparison should be allocated to comparative legal history or the sociology of law, not to comparative law.[32] Specifically, there are three principal points urged by the methodologists: (1) that the results obtained by use of the comparative method should not be confused with the method; (2) that the results may contribute to comparative legal history or the sociology of law or to a deepened understanding of a branch of positive law, but they are not comparative law;[33] and (3) implied in this argument is a challenge to those who reject the methodologists' theory to prove that comparative law has an independent status.[34]

The first point may be readily granted. Although there is a jurisprudential view to the effect that substantive law is ultimately procedural[35] in that it tells people how to act, the difference between substance and procedure, between method and the acquired substantive knowledge, is deeply rooted; and for the present purpose, at least, its validity may be assumed.

The second thesis, however, raises several difficult questions. One phase of it can be disposed of briefly, namely, the argument that the many purposes of comparative study and the many uses to which it may be put support the theory that comparative law is only a method. The facts may be readily granted since it is evident that the motives of comparatists are diverse and that practical purposes such as improvement of legislation and the needs of lawyers are served and, also, that theoretical gains, for example, a better understanding of one's law and progress in juris-prudence and history, are achieved by use of comparative stud-ies. But the above interpretation is inadmissible since a body of knowledge must be distinguished from the motives of scientists and from the uses to which that knowledge is put, as is readily seen by reference to physics or chemistry. There are many mo-tives to stimulate scientific research and there are many practical and theoretical uses to which the "results" of the research are put. But no one, except some very subtle philosophers of science, de-nies that these are bodies of knowledge or argues that because of the diversity of their uses, these sciences comprise only methods of research. Unfortunately, at present, the results of comparative legal study do not find a ready place among existing sciences or disciplines. The actual problem implicit in the above argument therefore concerns the difficulty of discovering any common characteristics among the results of comparative study, and this is aggravated by the uncertainties of the "sociology of law."

The second point, moreover, rests upon the prior assumption —that comparative law is only the method of comparison. If, for example, it were assumed that physics was *only* scientific method, the knowledge acquired by the use of that method should, on that premise, be called something other than "physics," if it is not to be entirely ignored. Every empirical science has its methods but this obviously would not support the thesis that physics, biol-ogy, and so on are *only* these methods. If "the comparative method" applied to law has produced any knowledge, it is that knowledge which is of primary importance and it is that knowl-edge which should determine the naming of the relevant disci-pline. As suggested above, what has barred easy conformity to the established practice in this regard is the uncertainty regarding the results of the comparative method applied to law, and, as we shall see, this involves very difficult problems of social science. But the fact that "legal sociology" may have pre-empted the name of this product does not support the thesis that comparative law is only a method. What is implied on this premise is that com-parative law is both a method and legal sociology.

All that remains then is a verbal question—in view of the fact that the knowledge acquired by the comparative method is allocated to the sociology of law, is it not confusing to call that knowledge, also, "comparative law"? If the problem is only a verbal one, all that is required to solve it is agreement on the meaning of "comparative law." One solution is to restrict that term to "the method of comparison" and use "sociology of law" to designate the knowledge acquired by use of the method. On the other hand, in view of the ambiguity of "comparative law" and of the paramount importance of the knowledge acquired, why not abandon that term entirely and speak only of the method or methods of legal sociology?

It requires little reflection, however, to discover that the major problems confronting comparatists cannot be solved by verbal conventions, although their utility should not be ignored, and that much more difficult questions must be dealt with. For example, is knowledge acquired in comparative legal study and, if so, is that knowledge part of the sociology of law or should it be distinguished from that discipline? The great merit of Gutteridge's theory, even if it cannot prevail, is that it stimulates those holding contrary views to explore these very important problems.

It is necessary, however, to recognize at the outset that there are limitations on any answer to these questions, which may reasonably be expected. The solution of the age-old problem of the classification of knowledge has eluded the sustained efforts of many scholars. We have only to think of the vastly increased difficulties that have arisen from the specialization of knowledge, the growth of many social disciplines, and their departmentalization in the universities since Locke tried to solve this problem, to appreciate the enormous difficulty, indeed, the impossibility, of discovering any firm classification of mutually exclusive sciences and social disciplines in which comparative law can be neatly placed. By like token, the significance of present classifications of sciences and social disciplines should not be exaggerated. Even in biology, where classification has been cultivated for centuries, major problems remain unsolved; [36] and the rise of new sciences, such as biochemistry, complicates existing classifications.

What is nonetheless of paramount importance is the existence of distinctive bodies of knowledge. The issue, moreover, that divides comparatists does not require that the perennial problem of the classification of all knowledge be solved. This issue arose from the claim that comparative law is only a method, and it is therefore sufficient to show, if that can be done, that there is certain knowledge acquired by the comparative method, even though opinions may differ as to whether that knowledge comprises a distinct discipline. It is hoped that the following chapters will make evident that much more is involved than a narrowly circumscribed issue among legal comparatists, that, indeed, the above problem, when its various implications are articulated, concerns the foundations of legal and social theory.

The direction I shall take in dealing with these problems can be indicated in a practical way by imagining that a social scientist who accepts the view of legal sociology or legal science, stated above, examined well-known studies of comparative law. Is it not extremely unlikely that he would find there the kind of knowledge he would expect to find in a social discipline such as the sociology of law, thus conceived? But if comparative law is not the sociology of law (legal science) in the above sense, then such an appraisal is misdirected; and we should consider an alternative to both of the above theories of comparative law. Before proceeding to do that, we can derive additional insight into this basic problem by placing the above theories of comparative law in the context of its history.

The Modern Origins of Comparative Law

Aristotle's *Constitution of Athens* is the most famous instance of the antiquity and universality of "the comparative method." But comparative legal scholarship, as a recognized profession carried on in many countries, is a modern achievement. There is some ground for setting its modern origin as early as the end of the sixteenth century, specifically in the work of Jean Bodin (1530–1596) [37] or in that of Leibnitz who, at an early age (1667), conceived a science of law in universal terms. But the usual preference is to fix the date of the beginning of modern comparative law at 1748, when Montesquieu's *The Spirit of Laws* was published. This has been challenged by Radbruch who, depreciating Montesquieu's "aprioristic manner, more inspired by politics than by science," maintained that it was the criminalist, Anselm Feuerbach (1755–1833) who founded modern comparative law. Radbruch refers particularly to Feuerbach's essay on the criminal science of the Koran, published in 1800.[38] In any case, it took many more years before comparative law became widely recognized as a type or branch of legal scholarship.

The first chair of comparative law seems to have been that at the Collège de France in 1832 [39] but the first major academic step, emphasized by French writers, was the chair in comparative criminal law established for Ortolan in the University of Paris in 1846.[40] Significant as this was for future progress, it symbolized far less than a general recognition of comparative law as a scholarly discipline. Pollock suggested 1869, the year when the Society of Comparative Legislation was organized in Paris and "Maine was appointed the first Professor of Historical and Comparative Jurisprudence at Oxford" as the time when "a new branch of legal science" was definitely recognized.[41] But in his *Village-Communities* (1871), Maine wrote that "the chief function of Comparative Jurisprudence is to facilitate legislation and the practical improvement of law," [42] which hardly indicates recognition of it as a science. In 1869 the French Society for Comparative Law was founded and similar British and German societies were organized in 1895; in Germany the journal for comparative and legal science had been established in 1881. In 1890 two chairs in Civil Law were allotted to comparative law at Paris, in 1892 comparative commercial law was added, and by 1895 comparative constitutional law was being taught in all the French faculties.[43] When the first International Congress of Comparative Law met in Paris in 1900, it was made quite clear there that comparative law had for some years been established as a legal discipline. At that meeting Pollock said, and Lambert agreed, "men now alive saw it born." [44]

The *Procès-Verbaux* of the meeting contain illuminating evidence of the theoretical foundations of the new discipline and of the intellectual background of these comparatists. It is plain that they were under the influence of Comte's sociology and the progress of biology, especially the theory of evolution.[45] Auspicious beginnings of the directly relevant disciplines had been made in ethnological jurisprudence, universal legal history, and comparative jurisprudence. Many of the participants in the 1900 meeting stated that the function of these disciplines was to trace the evolution of various societies and, finally, of all mankind through a series of definite stages. Comparative jurisprudence and universal legal history were identified with comparative law and legal sociology, although an occasional dissenter sought distinctions among them, one of the more interesting ones being to the effect that comparative law should only collect the facts of legal evolution while sociology had the scientific task of discovering the general laws which these data expressed. Lambert was the general reporter of the Congress, and his summary of the special reports makes it quite clear that by 1900 comparative law was regarded as a social science. Comparative law, he said, had the mission of discovering the natural laws of the development of the legal life of society, *"la vie juridique."* [46] In opposition to the suggestion that comparative law only collected facts while sociology used them to discover the relevant natural laws, Lambert asked whether comparative law, viewed as a science of the manifestations of *la vie juridique*, was not itself the sociology of law. [47]

But he also insisted that there was another kind or branch of comparative law, having a wholly different purpose, namely, to effect the *"rapprochement,"* not the mere juxtaposition, of the common elements of the laws of the various legal systems. He pointed, for example, to the derivation of a single body of law from French and German collections of customary laws in his argument that this type of comparative law dated from the Roman *ius gentium.* [48] Saleilles called it *"droit commun législatif";* but he was particularly interested in "the progress of universal legislation," *"droit commun de l'humanité,"* reflecting a natural law perspective. [49] As stated, however, the principal emphasis in the meeting was on comparative law viewed as a social science, even then called the sociology of law. In terms of the kind of knowledge to be acquired, the emphasis was placed on the evolution of legal institutions and on relevant trends and causes.

The present identification of comparative law with legal sociology is thus in the direct line of descent from the dominant view held by the comparatists of 1900. This does not mean that there have been no important changes in the theory of legal sociology since 1900 or that scholars standing in that tradition are bound by the then-prevailing views regarding that discipline. It is a curious fact, for instance, that Lambert did not mention his contemporary who became the master of French sociology, Emile Durkheim, although *De la division du travail social* had appeared in 1893 and *Les règles de la méthode sociologique* in 1895. He and Max Weber have become dominant influences in contemporary sociology. Many other important changes have occurred. For example, ethnological jurisprudence has made way for a much more critical legal anthropology, and the comparative method of universal history and the theory of unilinear progress have been abandoned.[50]

Nevertheless, what bulks large in the foundation of the above theories of comparative law is the enormous influence of nineteenth-century sociology on the Continental scholars and the lack of that influence on Gutteridge. Bryce had treated "the comparative method" as one of the methods of legal science. "Legal science" for him, however, was not the sociology of law, but a juridical "science directed to practice. . . ."; and the utility of its method was "in producing a system of law. . . ." Thus, too, he found the essential character of social and political science not in the nature of the subject matter or in that of the relevant knowledge but in "its method." He found theoretical significance in the comparative method only when it was used in history. Like Lambert, he emphasized common legal conceptions, and what the former referred to as *rapprochement*, Bryce called the "identity of substance under diversity of description."[51]

In the 1900 meeting at Paris, Pollock, Bryce's contemporary, formulated the thesis quoted above, that comparative law is not itself a science, but is only the method of comparison applied to law. In a later essay, Pollock wrote of "the comparative method," "comparative enquiry," and "comparative research."[52] Yet he criticized Maine for the latter's failure to see, as late as 1871, that the comparative method had more than practical utility for legislation.[53] He also linked the comparative to the historical method which, he, too, believed, led to results that had theoretical significance. But despite his references to Montesquieu, Vico and

Amari, Pollock hardly did more than hint at the theoretical significance of comparative law.

Besides these antecedents, there was much within Gutteridge's own observation that might have led him to take a skeptical view of the sociology of law, as it had been conceived. The enormous expansion of social studies had not, nor has it yet, produced a firm body of knowledge which approximates physical science. The debates on methods continue interminably, as does that on the nature of the subject matter and the kind of knowledge that should be sought.[54] If we are to do justice to Gutteridge's view of comparative law, we must bear these facts in mind. Indeed, the dominant theory in the 1900 Congress, reflecting the belief in unilinear evolution, a universal legal history built on that presupposition, and the "vague generalities" of sociology,[55] must have rung hollow in the ears of many social scientists thirty years later. In these circumstances, it is noteworthy that Gutteridge emphasized the importance of the social context and the function of laws. At the same time, however, while Gutteridge's dedication to the detailed scholarship that must be carried on, if comparative law is to command respect, places his successors in his debt, it is in the realm of social theory, including the relevant jurisprudence, that the question of the nature of comparative law must be determined.

The doubts raised above regarding "the comparative method" are fully confirmed in the history of the social sciences since Comte. Comte discussed various methods of study in relation to his theory of the progress of thought from theology to metaphysics to positivist science; and he related the methods of observation, experiment, and comparison to "social physics" and also referred to the historical method.[56]

The first book in English to use the term "comparative politics" was by Edward A. Freeman, and his enthusiasm for "the comparative method" was unbounded. Influenced by biology and anthropology, he wished to discover the common origins of similar political institutions,[57] and his immediate successors combined that genetic interest with the historical method and the analysis of concepts.[58] With the ascendency of physics in the esteem of later social scientists, "the comparative method" came to be associated or identified with "scientific method" and with systematic, theoretical, rather than genetic, explanation. At present, among scientifically oriented political scientists, "comparative politics" is practically synonymous with "political science." [59] The only purpose served by "comparative" seems to be to indicate an interest in the study of foreign governments [60] and in models, systems, and other modes of rigorously scientific thought; for example, books bearing the label "comparative politics" use the concepts, terms, and theories of scientifically oriented political science, and no important difference is discernible. The term "comparative politics" has recently been criticized on the ground that the study of foreign governments is fallaciously taken to mean that the method is "automatically comparative" and to imply that comparative study requires the use of foreign data.[61]

Many terms have been used to designate the methods of scholarly investigation: a priori, a posteriori, deductive, inductive, analogical, historical,[62] artistic, genetic, statistical, scientific, intuitive, observation, experiment, classifying, hypothesizing, empirical, logical, ethical, quantitative, descriptive, narrative, dialectical, codifying, and so on.[63] Comparison is involved in all these methods. It is characteristic of all intellectual functions whose purpose is the discovery of sameness and difference. John Dewey summed up the matter as follows: "Comparison is a name for *all* operations in which identities and incompatibilities in evidential force are determined. It is a name for any and all of the operations by means of which alleged or provisional data are determined to *be* data with respect to the problem set by a given indeterminate situation; by which some facts are determined to be the 'facts of the case' in hand and other facts not to be. . . . It is a blanket term for the entire complex of operations by which some existences are selectively instituted as data and other existential materials are eliminated as having nothing to do with the case. . . ." [64]

"Comparative" is deemed superfluous by sociologists and by scholars of "comparative religion." [65] "Comparative psychology" is said to be "synonymous with animal psychology" and to imply "scientific study." [66] Especially significant is the fact that "comparative philology" has become simply "linguistics." Finally, the science which stimulated comparison more than any other influence was and continues to be "biology," not "comparative biology," and this is also true of anthropology.[67] But, it may be added, the fact that past uses of the terms "comparative" and "the comparative method" are seriously questionable on theoretical grounds does not exclude their use as a convenient reference to the interests noted above and to others to be discussed later.

Thus the principal course of the following discussion has been charted. Believing it is important to determine what, if anything, is distinctive about comparative law, and unable, for the reasons stated above, to accept the theory that comparative law is *only* the method of comparison, we have charted our course in the direction of past and possible results of comparative study, with a view to discovering distinctive knowledge there. We have been particularly aided by discussions of comparative law in terms of "function," "social context," "institution," and the "sociology of law" to look in the direction of social science to find the solution of our inquiry.

2

THE SOCIOLOGY OF LAW

That the so-called "result" of the comparative method, applied to law, is a kind of knowledge, indeed, a social discipline, is the position of those who hold that comparative law is a synonym of legal sociology and legal science. Some questions were raised about this in the first chapter; but a theory which has been supported by many distinguished comparatists from 1900 to the present time merits detailed consideration.

Comte's *Positive Philosophy* (1830–1842), which greatly influenced the early comparatists, barely mentions positive law; and despite the significance of the work of Montesquieu and Feuerbach, it may be doubted whether they contributed more than initial insights regarding a science of law. More important was the rise of the German historical school, represented in Savigny's jurisprudence establishing the connectedness of past and present legal institutions and laying the foundations of the theory that law is a cultural fact. Jhering's *Geist des römischen Rechts* (1852–1865) was a brilliant landmark. But, again, it was not until the end of the nineteenth century that the sociology of law became a recognized discipline, coinciding with the rise of modern anthropology, political and other social science. As was seen above, for instance in the work of Maine, the temporal concurrence of comparative law and legal sociology was not fortuitous.

A thorough inquiry into the sociology of law would deal not only with the nineteenth-century pioneers in legal science and the early comparatists already mentioned but, also, and much more fully, with the work of Ehrlich, Petrazhitsky and his successors, Gurvitch and Sorokin, Durkheim and his disciple Duguit,

Max Weber, the French Institutionalists, *Interessenjurisprudenz,* Horváth, Pound, the American and Scandinavian Realists, and with the work of other scholars who have made important contributions to this branch of jurisprudence.[1] It is impossible here to discuss even the principal issues in these theories of legal sociology; we shall have to strike directly at the core of what is most important in the present inquiry.

Generality of Legal Sociology

If we accept the early comparatists' (and perhaps the still-prevailing) view, that the sociology of law consists, or will consist, of universal generalizations,[2] we must keep in mind, as a necessary point of reference, the model of that theory, the structure of physical science.[3] For example, the law that gases expand in direct proportion to increase in temperature and inversely as to increase in pressure, manifests the following characteristics. First, in its inclusive reference to "all gases," the law generalizes beyond the known and even the knowable data. Although scientists have not and never will be able to test every gas in the universe, the generalization is universal. Second, the generalization is based on data it describes, and if the scientist is challenged, he can produce factual evidence to verify the law. Third, the law expresses a covariation of certain variables—the volume of gas in one wing of the generalization and the temperature in the other. As the one changes, so correspondingly, does the other. Fourth, the compendency of physical laws interconnects them by common terms to form a system of ideas, giving physical science its formal character and making deductive manipulation both possible and extremely significant. There are also very abstract theories in physical science which are not empirically verifiable, and some philosophers hold that science consists only of methodological principles. We cannot discuss the niceties of these issues [4] but the above summary of the prevailing view of salient features of physical science will serve the present purpose.

If we examine the literature of the sociology of law, we also find various generalizations there. For example, there is Weber's generalization of the evolution from charismatic to rational authority. There is Maine's generalization of the chronological order of legal growth—themistes, unwritten case law interpreted by an elite, codification, fiction, equity, and legislation. And there is also Maine's better known, though more challenged, generalization, that the law of progressive societies has evolved from a law of status to that of contract. One of Durkheim's generalizations is that the evolution of law, coinciding with the transformation of primitive, "mechanical" society into complex "organic" societies, specialized by the division of labor, has been from criminal law to restitutive law. There are generalizations of "universal legal history" and early anthropology in terms of development from communism to private property, from feud to punishment by organized political society, from matriarchal to patriarchal law, from endogamy to exogamy, from polygamy to monogamy, from mass community to forms of individualistic society.[5] Many similar generalizations could be marshalled concerning stages of social and legal evolution—Bücher: hunting and fishing, pastoral, agricultural, commercial, industrial, financial, and governmental economies; Kovalevsky: horde, gens, patriarchal nomadism, feudalism and democracy; and Pound: primitive or archaic law, strict law, equity (Natural Law), the maturity of law, and the socialization of law.[6] We are not here concerned with the validity of these generalizations (physical science, too, has its share of error) but, instead, with the distinctive structure of the sociology of law viewed as a type of general knowledge. In this regard, it will have been noticed that the above generalizations are in terms of trends, not of co-variation. The influence of biology is evident.

In order to provide some definite illustrations of the structure of current legal sociology which approximates that of physical science more closely, I shall, with the reader's indulgence, very briefly summarize some conclusions of my research on the law of theft.[7] Important changes in this branch of criminal law, as it evolved in England, were found to be definitely related to certain economic changes associated with the commercial and, especially, the industrial revolution. For example, the law of embezzlement was greatly influenced by the rise of banking. The modern law of criminal fraud was similarly related to popular dealing in stocks and the subsequent bursting of bubbles. A whole series of reforms in the law of larceny was connected with other economic changes; and the rise of the modern law of receiving stolen property, as distinguished from the earlier law of mere accessoryship after-the-fact to larceny, was likewise explained. This sort of influence was described in some detail but the relations of the reform of the law and the economic changes were not precisely formulated. More definite generalizations concerned functional relations of social problems, current law, and judicial administration, and the temporal order of (1) recognition of a social problem, (2) official practices designed to adapt the law to the current need, and (3) legislation. The rise and uses of technicality in the above context were also discussed.

Of particular relevance are certain other conclusions stated in a more significant form. For example, it was found that the rate of automobile theft varies directly in proportion to the size of cities, that is, given a number of cities arranged in the order of the size of their population, the rate of automobile theft per unit of population increases with increase in the population of the cities. It was found, on the other hand, that the rate of arrests for automobile theft is in inverse proportion to the size of the population. In the study of embezzlement, it was quickly discovered that relatively few prosecutions are initiated (even where there is ample evidence to convict) in proportion to the vast number of known embezzlers. Specifically, it was found that the rate of prosecution varies directly in proportion to the amount embezzled and the amount of publicity given the defalcations and that it varies inversely in relation to restitution and the degree of psychological identification of employer with embezzler.

These generalizations, it will have been noticed, resemble scientific laws in certain ways. They are stated in the form of universal propositions, not limited to particular data, as are statistical descriptions. They rest on definite factual evidence. And they express a co-variation of variables—the rate of automobile theft or of arrests, in the one wing, in relation to size of population, in the other, and the rate of prosecution for embezzlement in relation to the variables noted above. Of course, these generalizations are not parts of a system of social laws, and there are other grounds upon which the indicated similarity of a segment of legal sociology and physical science may be disputed. For example, it may be urged that exceptions to every sociological generalization can be discovered and that, because of the nature of the data, any significant social science generalization must be statistical rather than universal. These and other problems concerning the nature of the social disciplines will be discussed later. Enough has been presented, it is hoped, to give definite meaning to the above comparatists' view of the "sociology of law"; and there may be some collateral gain in advancing from speculation about the possibility of a sociology of law to the exhibition of the above findings—generalizations of trends and of co-variation which, few as they are, give evidence of the feasibility of constructing such a discipline.

In emphasizing these generalizations of the sociology of law, it is not implied that there are no important differences between social and physical science. Nor is it suggested that the most defensible theory of the sociology of law views it as comprised of general knowledge modeled after physical science. This problem will be discussed later.[8] But it has been necessary to avoid terminological quagmires by focusing the discussion, first, on the theory of legal sociology maintained among legal comparatists and many social scientists, especially in the United States.

The sociology of law, thus viewed, consists of distinctive general descriptions of social data which are experienced as specific facts and events. Each datum, event, or action occurs at a certain time and place and under particular circumstances. The discovery of significant uniformities among these diverse data is the purpose of scientific research. But the condition of the success of the scientific enterprise is completely to ignore the unique characteristics of the data, the differences among them.[9]

Knowledge of Individuality—Art and History

However valuable science may be, it is far from being the only kind of knowledge there is. There is also, for instance, the specific knowledge we have of ourselves and of other persons, which sometimes reaches the point where very accurate predictions can be made of what will be done in certain situations. This is part of the layman's common sense, and its admission into the realm of knowledge is warranted by the reliability of its guidance in everyday living. There is, also, the deeper knowledge of individuals which psychiatrists acquire in the course of clinical and analytical diagnoses.

It is in this especially meaningful realm of knowledge of individuality that art and history find their expression, much of art representing this realm subvocally by sounds or colors arranged in harmonious forms, while history describes and explains the course of unique events. Many barbs have been directed at both. For example, it has been said that the only thing we learn from history is that we don't learn from history; and anyone who has visited museums of modern art must have been puzzled by some of the paintings. But we are not required to call every drawing a work of art or to believe that every book labelled "history" is the product of scholarship. Knowledge consists of truths validated in correspondence to reality and in coherence with other tested propositions. That art says something about reality is evidenced not only by the wide appreciation and survival of genuine works of art but also by apt criticism of them in terms of their authenticity, coherence, suggestiveness, and so on.[10] Dewey points out that "thinking consists in ordering a variety of meanings" of the world and that this "is the essence of fine art." [11] In sum, while the scientist deals with general patterns, the artist is concerned with particularity. More than any other medium, art expresses unique truths wrapped in feeling and imagination.[12]

History shares with art this concern with individuality; indeed, "individuality and progress are names for the historical aspect of existence." [13] Perhaps the widest agreement among comparatists of all persuasions is that history is not merely a helpful adjunct, it is essential in comparative law.[14] The importance of the subject suggests that we consider some pertinent facts.

What the historian does, in brief, is to reconstruct past events with all the art and accuracy he commands, describing the actors, their motives, and their situation. He tells what important changes occurred between two points of time. The reader participates vicariously in the experience of events that may have occurred long ago and far away and he comes appreciably to understand the persons whose roles he plays, especially what was behind and in the context of their action, why they acted as they did, and what happened at particular times and places. There is, no doubt, a degree of self-deception in any belief that one can "fully" re-create and re-live a long bygone event, take the roles of the different actors, some of whom may be strange to his traditions, and experience what the participants actually experienced.[15] That is why good historians describe the relevant social context and external conditions in detail, to guide and inform the reader's insight into what happened.[16] But unless the present is an illusion, history is not fiction. There are historical truths no less than scientific and artistic truths.

Actions and events having legal significance also occur as particulars. Certain individuals do this or that to or with other individuals at specific times and places. A subsequent litigation is inevitably unique in some degree, and a particular judge, different in some ways from all other judges, renders a decision which, in some respect, is unlike all other decisions. It is true, of course, that one's understanding of any legal event and of the actors in it depends in large measure upon his general knowledge of such matters, for example, his knowledge of law and human nature. But this only implies that socio-legal events and the participants in them also have general aspects or, if one prefers, that there are different ways of looking at events and persons. One may thus imagine a range in the types of knowledge, extending from knowledge of the unique character of events, such as art and history provide, to the most general knowledge of those events, expressed in science. This differs from the Stoic classification—logic, ethics, and physics (empirical knowledge)—and from a recent functional view that knowledge consists of "vision, interpretation and criticism, and science." [17] In the present discussion, knowledge is viewed in terms of its structure, especially its range from knowledge of individuality to that expressed in universal generalizations.

History, of course, employs concepts and other generalizations, just as ordinary speech is perforce expressed in nouns and other word-forms that refer to classes—"revolution," "nation," "the French people." So, too, many historians are well versed in social theory, the hypotheses elaborated in the work of Marx, Spengler, and Toynbee, and other general patterns which great historians have woven into the fabric of their narratives.

But the historian's function is to describe the uniqueness of persons and events in a series of changes, to hold fast, say, to the distinctive concatenation of events called "the French Revolution" and to the personality of the one and only Napoleon in all history.[18] The historian's "compulsion [is] to give particular life to general abstractions . . . The historian then deals with precisely those intangible motions of men which cannot be captured in stable concepts. . . ." [19] It is not his concern to establish the validity of trend and causal generalizations. Unlike the sociologist, he captures the indeterminacy of the flow of events, not their destined march to a fixed end. He explains the nature of existing institutions by showing the growth of past events into those present forms, that is, by revealing that aspect of things, "the nature of which is . . . just their concrete history." [20] As the nature of a tree is shown in the very process of the change from seed to tree, so we understand an institution by tracing the steps whereby it came to be what it is and recognizing, at the same time, its bent towards future changes.[21]

Many of the differences in historical writing can be accounted for in terms of changing conceptions of what is important. One such change has been the shift from concentration on politics to the inclusion of a wider social and economic context. Given the turn of events, cultural factors are presently esteemed. What this implies for legal history is a shift from exclusive treatment of statutes and decisions to interpretations which set these laws in social contexts, in short, cultural legal history.[22] Among comparatists, where the significance of the social context is widely recognized, the need to produce cultural legal histories seems evident. A cultural legal history would deal not only with legal concepts but also with relevant social problems, values, contexts, and functions. But, as seen, its concern is with the individuality of its subject matter.

The above interpretation of history contrasts with a current theory to the effect that every occurrence, no matter how minute, can be understood as an instance of a relevant causal law.[23]

Applied to law, however, this theory immediately encounters serious difficulty, for example, when one considers the contributions of great judges—since their greatness inheres in their being exceptional. Discovery, problem-solving, and invention are what they are precisely because they are not mere instances of how things generally happen. The fact seems to be that placing particular events within a generalization provides an entirely different kind of explanation than history gives. It does not show the teleology of particular changes as solutions of problems. We wish to know, then, not only that economic changes and legal changes can be correlated in general descriptions but also for what reasons and through which steps the first general embezzlement statute, for example, came to be passed in England in 1799. We seek to understand current law by following the various stages of its development from a persuasive point of origin through a series of cogent changes, until we see how it came to be what it is.[24] If we have that kind of knowledge, we understand the law much better than we do if we know only that it is an instance of the general operation of economic or political forces.

"In order to know what it [the law] is," said Holmes, "we must know what it has been, and what it tends to become." [25] Historical research, therefore, presupposes "sufficient" knowledge of the selected existences to permit their delineation to a degree necessary for the conduct of inquiry to broaden and deepen knowledge of them. Since existing institutions have grown from past ones, our knowledge of both is a correlative affair; and excavations, the discovery of lost papyri, and other historical research sometimes shed new illumination on the present situation.

What distinguishes the historical research of the legal comparatist from that of other historians is that his present datum consists of common legal concepts and common legal institutions which determine his objective. A common concept or institution is always in his mind's eye as he probes the past to discover an apt origin, the stages in the development of that notion or institution as well as the particular divergencies that account for the differences among the respective systems. The tracing of much of American law to English common law is so habitual as to obscure the fact that present similarities are explained by use of the historical method. Common aspects of Continental systems are often traced to their origin in Roman law. The resemblance of Japanese criminal law, first to French, then to German, and later to American criminal law, and continuing traces of each influence are explained by reference to certain events and particular Frenchmen, Germans, and Americans who helped to introduce various parts of their criminal law into Japanese law. Given the resemblance, the differences among the laws must, of course, be accounted for, and that is, also, a function of the comparatist's historical research.

The area of imitation is vast, as is evident by mere reference to the influence of Roman law, canon law, law merchant, the adoption of English law in India and elsewhere, and numerous borrowings from American law by many nations, especially during the past hundred years. It is possible to go further than that and discover the origin of common legal concepts (as the principles of criminal liability) in certain moral ideas. While Greek philosophy, for example, may not have directly influenced Roman law, it provided a large store of ideas upon which many legal systems have drawn, frequently through channels not obviously associated with their source. But one need only glance at many laws of the American colonies to recognize their Biblical origin.

There are, however, other large areas of common legal concepts and institutions concerning which it seems unlikely that historical research can uncover a single source, and where, on other grounds, the theory of imitation is implausible. Many laws concern the elementary factors necessary for the survival of a society: the prohibition of violence, the care of women and children, provision for marriage, transmission of tradition, and the like. Here, it is not a common origin or the diffusion and imitation of laws but independent invention or discovery of a similar concept, legal solution, or institution that must be accounted for. The historical method can provide relevant facts—where and under what conditions similar concepts and institutions were invented; and it also facilitates the work of legal sociologists seeking answers in terms of general knowledge of common problems, common environments, common human nature, and whatever other theories guide social research. Frequently, there is an intermingling of imitation and invention, a general notion providing the starting point, but inventive adaptiveness supplying more definite articulations. Again, rudimentary ideas may have been invented but, with subsequent cultural contacts, they are modified and readapted.

In historical investigation, a philosophy is more or less clearly revealed. A Marxist will concentrate on changes in production and class structure, a Carlyle will study greatness among lawgivers, an idealist will center on spiritual factors, and those who share the writer's perspective will look for a plurality of causes and seek a balance between human initiative and inventiveness and the impact of the environment. Our present concern is not to consider the effect of the philosophies that guide the comparatist's historical research or to imply that "ideological" influence excludes the possibility of approximating "the truth," but to apprehend the character and functions of history, especially to emphasize what sets the legal comparatist apart from other historians. The datum that guides his study of the past, the present that he wishes to understand and explain, is a common legal concept or legal institution.

Thus, we may conclude that although events can be "fully" understood only if their general patterns are also considered, such general knowledge may supplement, but it cannot displace, historical knowledge. It barely touches the rich detail, the creativeness, the accidents and peculiar combinations of fact, as well as the sense of change in time that is significant in those events. A great deal inevitably escapes science that artists, historians, psychiatrists, political scientists, and perceptive laymen find important and dependable for many purposes. Indeed, in the human realm, this type of knowledge, which takes account of motivation and end-seeking, is more significant than knowledge of the common patterns of actions and events expressed in wide generalizations. Both types of knowledge are valuable, of course, and they are also compatible, since the one supplements the other. Accordingly, although emphasis upon knowledge of individuality is necessary to offset the current claim that science is the only kind of knowledge, it should not be forgotten that wider generalizations have an important, if presently modest, place in the social disciplines, including the sociology of law.

A Preliminary Statement of a Theory

We have reached the point in this discussion where it is possible to make a preliminary statement of a principal thesis of this book. *Comparative law is a composite of social knowledge of positive law, distinguished by the fact that, in its general aspect, it is intermediate between the knowledge of particular laws and legal institutions, on the one side, and the universal knowledge of them at the other extreme.* Comparative law is thus a halfway house. In its general aspect it goes beyond the knowledge of the single law or institution. But with reference to the other pole, while the sociology of law (legal science) generalizes over all law, comparative law is limited to a small number of laws and legal institutions.[26] This theory [27] accords with the fact that legal comparatists usually study parts of the law of a few countries, perhaps two or three, not what is common to all legal systems.[28] The conclusions typically reached in comparative legal study can be restated in the following form—in these two or three countries, the problems consisted of such and such common elements, the social contexts contained the following common features, common concepts A, B, C were found, the relevant trends and interrelationships were such and such, and so on.[29] While these conclusions might sometimes be helpful in the construction and verification of wider generalizations, it might also happen that they would not be applicable to other societies.[30]

The above statement that legal comparatists usually study parts of the law of very few countries should not be taken "too literally," nor are the "universal" generalizations of Maine, Pound, Wigmore, and others depreciated. This statement is intended to emphasize that, in the writer's view, current comparative law [31] is apt to be intensive study of narrow segments of law and, especially, that such study comprises a distinctive field of scholarship.

It is, of course, possible to generalize universally even on the basis of study of one datum. A classical case is Durkheim's *The Elementary Forms of the Religious Life.* Anticipating that his very general conclusions might be criticized because they were based on study of the religion of a single primitive people, Durkheim defends their validity by arguing that "the most characteristic elements of the religious life" were found there in an uncomplicated form.[32] Proceeding on similar premises with reference to the essentials of "legal order" or the functions of cultural practices and institutions to satisfy the basic needs of any society, it might be possible to generalize the results in very wide terms. What is here submitted is that statements of common concepts, trends and interrelations which are limited to very few bodies of law represent a very different kind of knowledge than do generalizations about all law. The point is not that the latter are apt to be invalid; and, admittedly, some of them are very significant. It is that, even though they are valid and represent a discovery of wider "sameness," they constitute a different type of social knowledge than do generalizations limited to very few data.

Perhaps the above thesis can be made more definite by bringing together some of the lines of the preceding discussion and adding relevant details. The first step in that direction requires that we hold before us a range of types of knowledge, extending from the extreme of knowledge of individuality (art and history) to that of the most general type of knowledge (physical science) with which the sociology of law was first associated in the above discussion. Comparative law was defined in terms of its relation to those "extreme types." If comparative law is taken to include cultural legal history, it consists, in part, of knowledge of individuality. The fact that this history leads to an increase in knowledge of common concepts and institutions does not make it any the less history. It is comprised of knowledge of unique origins and particular changes occurring in distinctive events at certain times and places—all focused on the current common datum. But this question of whether cultural legal history is part of, or ancillary to, comparative law may be set aside as largely one for conventional decision, leaving what is, in any case, most distinctive about comparative law—its limited generalizations in terms of concepts, trends, and interrelations common to laws of a very few countries.

Some may believe that there is no important difference between the limited generalizing described above and the universal generalization of physical science and rigorous social science. Science is knowledge of "sameness" and in a rigorously scientific perspective, the more "sameness" that is discovered, the better the knowledge; and, in any case, are not the two made of the same cloth? Attention may also be directed to biology and geology, which include many limited generalizations. And it may be further urged that the only reason the legal comparatist limits his general concepts and the findings of his research to the law of two or three countries is that that is as far as he has gone in his studies, implying that a future, highly improved comparative law will generalize in terms of all legal systems.

It must, of course, be recognized that "science" is an ambiguous term and that biology and geology are usually considered sciences. In terms of the present theory, this implies that comparative law is much closer to the kind of knowledge found in biology and geology than it is to that found in physics; indeed, it might be rewarding if comparatists of a sociological persuasion studied the structure of biology, especially its classifications, rather than the model of physical science. What is particularly important, however, is not the various senses in which "science" is used. The pertinent questions are whether valid distinctions can be made among types of knowledge on the basis of the chosen criterion—the range from knowledge of individuality to universal generalization—and if comparative law is significantly located between the indicated limits. Would the "perfect" legal comparatist or a group of legal comparatists who pooled their knowledge be transformed into legal or social scientists in the rigorous sense? Would they abandon the kind of work they now do and concentrate on high-level generalizations in the form of those found in physical science?

The answer, it is submitted, is that their present vocation is distinctive and valuable, not a mere expediency. One immediate evidence of this is the dependence of comparatists upon history and the fact that they are also bound to study and describe the differences among laws. A chemist does not hesitate to generalize universally regarding certain characteristics of gases even though he knows that chemists have examined only a minute fraction of them. He has no reason to suspect that the untested gases may be significantly different as regards the selected property. But a legal comparatist does not generalize regarding all laws. The differences among laws are important not only in discovering and delineating what is common in them but also in gaining additional insight into the relevant social actions, problems, and solutions. Differences are, of course, excluded from generalization, which subsumes only what is common.[33]

But the principal issue concerns the limited generalizations of the legal comparatist as contrasted with the "universal" generalizations of the "complete scientist." The legal comparatist's generalizations are not only limited to the law of very few countries, but he also takes many criteria into account, that is, the patterns he discovers tend to be complicated ones. The physical scientist not only generalizes "universally," that is, at a very high level, but he also takes account of only very few variables. Physical science is high-level generalization that says relatively few things about a vast number of particulars, while comparative law says relatively many things about a few data. It is as if one first compared two men and then, all men. The two men might reveal a hundred similar traits, but if one sought to discover what is common among all men by studying a carefully selected representative sample of them, he might be hard put to discover more than half a dozen such traits. Thus, as regards "all positive laws," the relatively few common conceptions elucidated in legal positivism are formulated at the highest level of legal abstraction. If one wishes to find common notions among a single branch of all legal systems, for instance penal law, he generalizes at a lower level necessary to preserve the distinctive character of the notions that comprise that branch of law. If he then compares English and French penal law, he finds, in addition to those common notions, many rules and doctrines that are shared by those systems.

What is involved, in sum, are different types and levels of generalization, required by important differences among the data and the kind of questions raised regarding the respective fields. Finally, we must recall that physical science abounds in knowledge expressed in significant quantitative terms and systematized to comprise theories that are deductively manipulable. There are, accordingly, several important differences between the knowledge of common concepts and institutions found among the laws of a few countries and the very general knowledge of which physical science is the model. The former does not reflect an inevitable or expedient limitation of knowledge but qualitative differences between human societies, laws and other artifacts, and the properties of physical and organic matter.[34] As was indicated above, in order to clarify current discussions of "comparative law," it was necessary in this chapter to fix a definite focal point of reference, and the "sociology of law" was therefore taken to mean the theory of comparatists and social scientists in the Comtean tradition, namely, generalizations of trends and, especially, universal generalizations in terms of covariations,[35] reflecting the model of physical science. But in the discussion of history and the differences among laws, in certain limited generalizations, and in reference to problem-solving, a more realistic sociology of law was indicated. This is also expressed in "case-history."

The sociological "case-history" is focused on an important event and a short span of time.[36] One writer used it in a study of the 1952 steel seizure case. Another presented a graphic case-history of a serious housing dispute in Illinois, involving the exclusion of Negroes from a public enterprise.[37] The psychiatric case-history has been mentioned.[38] A trial sometimes portrays a very effective case-history, which may be more systematically developed in a pre-sentence hearing. As counsel reconstruct the leading facets of the situation and delineate the roles and personalities of the actors, those who witness this come to feel as though they are actually participating in the dramatic occurrence. That is why juries sometimes reach verdicts which surprise persons who were not present at the trials. In recent years, a substantial literature has been written by political scientists, especially about Supreme Court decisions, in which the case-history was employed.[39]

Since this method of analysis seems very promising for comparative study, it may be helpful to summarize a relevant instance, a case-history of the Carrier's Case.[40] In this fifteenth-century English case, which concerned the consignment of certain bales of merchandise to be carried to Southampton, apparently for shipment abroad, the carrier broke open the bales and took some of their contents. In his subsequent trial for felony, the defense submitted that a trespass in getting possession was essential and, except for the Chancellor, who thought the case should be governed by natural law, this was acknowledged by the Bench to be a correct statement of the law. After various alternatives had been presented and rejected, an imaginative judge suggested that when the bales were broken into, the consignment terminated, and that, in legal effect, the consignor was reinvested with their possession—hence, taking the contents of the bales was a trespass. The conviction for felony was upheld and the law of larceny was enlarged, as legal scholars agree.

The pertinent question is how can one understand and explain this important legal change? An answer was sought in a case-history in which the law and its social context would be carefully interrelated. For various reasons it seemed probable that the bales contained wool, the product of the largest industry in England at that time. The needs of the dawning commercial age were explored, including the economic interests of the king, who was, himself, a trader and in considerable debt to the Hanseatic merchants. The likelihood of royal pressure on the judges was increased by the subservience of the judiciary—Coke's courageous challenge lay two centuries ahead. On the directly legal side, there was the infrequency of parliamentary sessions and the availability of only a single effective sanction, so that the choice was limited to conviction of the felony or no legal solution of the problem. While there were precedents supporting the defense, they had not yet crystallized into the tough law of a later day. Each of the indicated types of social influence was described in some detail with a view to achieving a realistic reconstruction that would permit the reader to visualize that important legal situation and see how the social problem was solved and why the solution took its particular direction.

Unlike the indeterminacy sustained in history, the case-history is sociological in intent, moving towards a fixed goal.[41] What also distinguishes it from traditional and cultural legal histories are compression of the events within a very short period of time and deliberate guidance by theories of social science. For example, the analysis of the Carrier's Case conformed to a pluralistic theory of social change in terms of the interaction of human resource-fulness and social context. On the other hand, general interrelations are not formulated in case-history, although they are much more definitely suggested than in historical narrative; and the purpose is, also, to increase insight into efforts to solve problems in a given social context. In sum, the comparison of case-histories may be added to cultural legal history and to knowledge of the limited generalizations previously discussed, to comprise a sociology of law that must be sharply contrasted with that of comparatists and others, modeled after physical science.

The respective theories of sociology are also sharply opposed. Some scholars argue that the most serious fallacy that can be made is to adopt the model of physical science in the study of human actions and culture. It is insisted that ideas, values, motivations, reasons, and end-seeking are distinctive and paramount. Knowledge of them consists largely of insight (*Verstehen*) derived in vicarious participation and tested and amplified by study of relevant external data.[42] A sociology of law, it is argued, cannot be constructed of universal generalizations of the co-variation of variables, which is apt only in physical science where one is perforce an external observer of inanimate data. The very possibility of discovering such causal laws is dismissed as illusory in light of the complex, value-laden nature of social relationships. The physical realm and the biological, in lesser degree, are of such natures as to lend themselves to relatively simple generalization in rigorous terms that are meaningful. But any effort to construct rigorously scientific theories of human actions and social relationships must fail because it would require a reduction of those complexities to such oversimplified terms as to be either insignificant or misleading.[43] What can and should be attended to, instead, is the kind of historical and intermediate knowledge indicated above in the discussion of the "results" of comparative study. This knowledge can be articulated in the analysis of problem-solving, in the description of legal rules and institutions in relation to their social contexts, in case-histories, in estimates of the functions that laws serve, and in other limited generalizations in terms of trends and interrelationships.

Hume, rather than Comte, is the founder of the opposed positivist social science, and Bentham's "felicific calculus" evidenced the persuasiveness of the argument that the "moral sciences" should be modeled after physics. The seventeenth-century revolution in that science joined the current of nineteenth-century progress in biology; and the social scientists of our generation are the heirs of both of these powerful movements in scientific thought. Able exponents of this perspective have rejected every one of the criticisms summarized above, and are committed to the construction of rigorously scientific social science.[44] The issues have been agitated in the United States for half a century, and both positions continue to be warmly defended by distinguished scholars.

It is submitted, with deference, that these issues cannot be resolved so long as they are carried on in terms of methodology without supporting illustrations of actual research conducted preferably by the protagonists themselves. If this were done, the polemics would take different, more fruitful directions. For example, it would be necessary to deal realistically with very significant social research which did not culminate in universal or statistical generalizations or in the long-hoped-for scientific theories. On the other hand, results of extant research, some of which were noted above, show that significant trends and patterns of the co-variation of variables, especially "middle-range" social laws, can be discovered. There is no reason why some social scientists should not seek such general knowledge while their colleagues remain interested in the narrower, more realistic types of knowledge discussed above.[45]

This does not imply that social generalizations are to be read as if they were laws of physics. The latter connote quantitative measurement and the determined movements of inanimate things. Neither of these characteristics is attributable to sociological generalizations. When the results reached concerning, say, prosecution for embezzlement are related to other "variables," this cannot be taken to mean that certain movements of human bodies are correlated as are precise degrees of temperature and volumes of gases. It is true, of course, that human action is far from being wholly free and that, instead, it is largely influenced by passion and unreason. But while this suggests certain analogies and supports arguments in terms of "the logic of science," it does not follow that significant, measurable co-variations are discoverable in interpersonal relations. Meaningful interrelated influences—efforts and factors—are indicated; and it may be suggested that anyone who has engaged seriously in social research will agree that it is no simple task to discover such general interrelations. As stated, such social generalizations must be read against the detailed description of the relevant efforts to solve particular problems, if they are to be significant.

By like token, it is fallacious to ignore the significance of generalization in the social disciplines on the ground that such statements necessarily imply the philosophy of physics, or to discount them as mere guesswork. It may, of course, be argued that there are always exceptions to any social law: the dubious validity of Durkheim's and Maine's generalizations can be adduced. The writer's simple generalizations regarding automobile theft and arrests for automobile theft in relation to the size of cities were based on American data during a limited period of years, and it may be discovered that these generalizations are not valid elsewhere or for other periods of time. The generalizations regarding prosecution for known embezzlement in relation to restitution probably rest on a firmer basis because they involve the rationality of reducing an economic loss. Still, their universal validity is uncertain because the postulation of "the same conditions" raises difficult problems in the social disciplines.[46] For example, although everyone wishes to avoid or reduce an economic loss, it is conceivable that governmental pressure or fear of sanctions or the ideal of civic duty has stimulated a different pattern of conduct. In any case, however, even if exceptions can be found, something very important may be signified in carefully formulated generalizations supported in detailed research. Indeed, some generalizations are essential to guide and lend significance to any social research.

For the reasons discussed above, however, the legal sociology espoused by comparatists in the Humean-Comtean tradition and by their scientific successors is remote from the work of legal comparatists. It is equally remote from the likelihood of early realization even two hundred years after Hume proposed that the "moral sciences" be reconstructed after the model of physical science. The respective types of research, temperament, and acquired knowledge differ so patently that whatever terminology is employed to designate various disciplines, those differences should be recognized.[47] In the present state of social theory it would be illusory to believe that general agreement on the future of social science can be reached, especially since the relevant influences are deeply rooted. But whatever the prospects of social science may be, it is possible to take account of extant types of knowledge, as has been attempted above, and to make that the basis for determining the province and nature of comparative law and related disciplines.

Certain definite conclusions are therefore indicated: first, if one holds fast to the scientific theory of legal sociology, suggested by Hume and Comte, which is to be modeled after physical science, it is impossible to establish that "comparative law" means that kind of knowledge. Comparative law is not a sociology or science of law expressed in universal causal generalizations that can be systematized; and the prospect of its becoming such a science is very remote. Second, comparative law may include cultural history focused on common legal concepts and institutions. Third, although certain wide generalizations, circumspectly interpreted and employed, have an important role to play, this type of knowledge differs sharply from current comparative scholarship, especially its central thrust characterized by its concern with differences, history, and limited generalizations. Fourth, if the sociology of law is given the more realistic interpretation suggested above, it may be called "normative" or "humanistic legal sociology" in contrast to "scientific legal sociology" or "legal science." Fifth, if "comparative law" is to be used as a convenient reference to the work of certain legal scholars, it should mean "conceptualist comparative law," to be discussed in the following chapter. These suggestions are offered in awareness of present, diverse terminologies, with a view to implementing, if only in slight degree, a long-hoped-for and much-needed uniformity of usage.

What has been allocated above to "humanistic legal sociology" may seem to be a heterogeneous mixture, not because scholars have different motives for their work or because what they discover can be put to various uses, but because no pattern unifying the knowledge of law and legal institutions has been discerned in the distinctive history, case-history, limited generalizations, and so on; indeed, no effort has, as yet, been made to accumulate the "results" of comparative legal scholarship. If such a pattern were constructed by the reduction of the above types of knowledge to a set of common terms which could be systematized, it would be dismissed as meaningless. But if what is intended is a single rationale and the consequent compatibility of these types of knowledge, that can be found in their relation to a common subject matter—positive law.

Before we can deal with that subject matter in the required sociological perspective, it is necessary to take due account of a third, important theory of comparative law—that concerned with "common concepts," the special province of the legal comparatist. It has, of course, been impossible to avoid some discussion of this theory, which is actually the hardest working member of the family of theories of comparative law. But we have reached the point where we must consider conceptualism in comparative law not only to elucidate its distinctive character but also to determine its place in humanistic legal sociology.

3

CONCEPTUALISM

While polemical writing has emphasized "the comparative method" and the sociology of law, the professional work of most legal comparatists has been devoted to the study of the rules of different legal systems with a view to discovering their similarities and differences.[1] "Common concept" has been the slogan of professional comparative study since the 1900 Paris Congress.[2]

As was previously indicated, however, "common concept" meant different things to those who used that term. Lambert viewed *droit commun législatif* as existing positive law,[3] and he took a practical view of its use.[4] For Saleilles, the sociology of law would consist of descriptive generalizations, while comparative law, being normative, sought to discover the best extant law in order to derive ideals which would give conscious direction to legal reform.[5] A very different kind of "common concept," also suggested at the 1900 Congress, meant the stages of social evolution through which all societies were supposed to pass and causal ideas employed in the relevant universal legal history. To this might be added the types of society which Tarde emphasized. Recently, Marc Ancel has suggested another "common concept" to be found in the trend of the "living law of our time," especially in the policy of the social legislation enacted in many countries during the past twenty-five years.[6] In sum, "common concept" has meant an identical or similar rule of positive law, a concept "covering phenomena of the different systems,"[7] the best rules, an ideal law suggested by them, a trend, and concepts found among socio-legal institutions. Perhaps all of these views were intended in a treatise which defines comparative law as an "independent dogmatic discipline," "*droit comparé dogmatique*," analogous to the "dogmatic," that is, analytical study of the concepts of municipal law. The purpose of this conceptualist discipline is to describe the common elements of modern civilized systems of law. It is also said to include the juxtaposition and comparison of their historical origins, sources, evolution, form, style, technique, method of application of their laws, and their solution of social and economic problems as well as critical evaluations.[8]

This mingling of legal and nonlegal common concepts is also found in "the unification movement." Unification, as the "process by which conflicting rules of two or more systems of law are replaced by a single rule," [9] implies that the new, common rule may differ from both of the conflicting rules; and in that case it could not be derived from them. This type of unification suggests a political movement, and that has met sharp criticism.[10] It should be distinguished from the *droit commun de l'humanité* which inspired Saleilles in 1900, when he anticipated present programs for world law.

These ideals have been criticized as utopian in view of conflicting economic interests, national policies, and the reluctance of people to abandon the law in which they see the embodiment of many national virtues.[11] In any case, the neglect of the differences among laws and legal systems is the particular point of recurrent criticism of movements for unification of law, which are viewed as escapes from the detailed study that is required if comparative law is to progress.[12]

In dealing with this criticism, Ancel has suggested that the movement for unification, as a political effort to secure the adoption of laws, should be distinguished from scientific unification, the product of analysis and synthesis of existing legal systems, which is the goal par excellence of comparative legal scholarship. At the same time, the two are not unrelated because appreciation of the scholar's achievement, especially of the revealed similarities among legal systems, would influence political action towards unification. The scholar's universalism, concludes M. Ancel, does not lead to a new natural law or a new *jus gentium* but to a *jus inter gentes,* a common language among jurists, a common meeting ground, and increased understanding of the common good.[13]

The above summary of a very extensive literature on the motif of conceptualist comparative law must suffice to indicate the range of relevant problems. The first step in the elucidation of these problems is, evidently, to try to make sense of the elusive "concept."

The Concept

One may believe that the concept is, at bottom, an insoluble mystery but if we do not lose sight of what is involved, namely, knowledge and the "realities" of the world, we can guide inquiry in the right directions. What should be particularly kept in mind is that philosophers have discussed and constructed many concepts, and that the history of jurisprudence, as an example, could be written in terms of different concepts of law. A concept of anything is thus an index of a theory of problems to be solved.

Presupposed in any concept is the intuitive recognition of the qualities of things;[14] to form a concept of anything is to apprehend what is "essential" in it ("John Smith is a man" implies recognition of an individual and the concept "man"). The two processes—recognition of qualities and apprehension of relevant concepts—are concomitant. The concept of any thing is the articulation of it in a context. The concept of red implies a range of colors, recognition of their qualities, comparison, and locating red in its proper place in the spectrum. From the very beginning of intelligibility, comparison is thus involved in conceptualization.

Every thing differs in some way from every other thing and, at the same time, any two things are alike in some respect. It can therefore be said that when two objects are compared, they participate in dozens of concepts or universals and, also, that some universals are found only in the one or the other object. To take account of the infinite variety of things in these terms would require rather awkward speech and, for ordinary purposes at any rate, one is warranted in recognizing degrees of "identity": "light green," "dark green," and so on.

Many philosophers have challenged the metaphysics of universals, maintaining that all that is involved is that things resemble each other in various respects and degrees. As children, we learn to recognize certain things and later to see that some things resemble them more or less while others are quite different. But although one may prefer that kind of language to discourse on universals, the fact is that things do have very pervasive qualities. The data of our experience have certain properties or characteristics and, in consequence of that, things resemble each other and some of them appear to be identical.[15] One may question the "universal" [16] and insist that it is the definition of classes that is decisive, but, like the rest of us, he allocates certain colored objects to the class of "red" or "green," and certain propositions to the class of positive law. These classifications are based on the given characteristics of things which must be taken account of regardless of one's linguistic preferences.[17]

To say that things resemble each other expresses a relation of those things to a shared property or quality. Which quality is chosen for comparison depends on the nature and purpose of an inquiry. For the purpose of traffic laws, red can tolerate a variety of pinks, lavenders, and maroons, while a painter has a wholly different problem and requires a much nicer classification. So, too, as we shall see, the various purposes of lawyers and scholars are reflected in correspondingly different concepts of law. In any case, resemblance implies difference—to say that two things resemble each other implies that they are also different.

Comparison implies inclusion within the same class; it implies that the members share at least one significant quality ("universal") in sufficient degree to warrant the instant interest. It is therefore impossible to compare, for example, apples and billiard balls with reference to vision or rationality or any other property which neither object has.[18] If "fruit" is the selected property, all that can be said is that apples are fruit and billiard balls are not fruit. Although comparison is involved in the relevant primitive recognition of these objects, "comparison" in a more sophisticated sense does not seem apt where there is only the placing of some objects within a certain class and the exclusion of others from it. In this sense, that is, as employed in various disciplines, comparability implies that the things compared are members of the same class.

If, however, two things appear to be exactly the same, as the color of postage stamps, we do not compare them, but only recognize an identical color.[19] This implies that only things that resemble each other—that are neither identical nor utterly different—are comparable. Thus, if we compare an apple and an orange, the quality being that of fruit, both objects are included in that class; and comparison consists of recognizing similarities and tolerated differences between the two items, differences which do not bar them from the class. This implies that the crucial question in the social disciplines concerns the selection of the criteria by reference to which classes are defined; we shall need to consider later what are the important characteristics of laws, in terms of which they can be significantly compared? These criteria, stipulated in a congruent "concept of law," are basic in any study of positive law.

Among comparable things, differences compatible with membership in the given class are as important as the similarities, indeed, these differences function to delineate the similarities. If the class is "human face," differences in size, shape, color, features, and so on are essential in determining what is a human face. As we come to know the differences better, we more clearly apprehend what is similar among the items of the class.

For example, with reference to the "initiation of criminal prosecutions," the actions of the officials and the respective institutions differ in various ways among legal systems. The prosecutor, judge in the preliminary hearing, and grand jury in the American system must be contrasted with the *procurator* and *juge d'instruction* in Continental systems in order to understand the similarities in the logic, meaning, and consequences of both processes. It is not simply that the differences in the respective institutions must be recognized and set aside in order to discover the common characteristics as residues. Our knowledge of the common traits of initiation of prosecution in various systems deepens with increased understanding of the differences in which the common pattern is expressed.[20] Since comparison implies resemblance, one can therefore think of comparison as the delineation of differences against a background of similarities. Although relevant differences are just as important in comparison as are similarities, it is also true that "the greater the resemblance the less the difference and vice versa." [21]

In sum, as will shortly become apparent, since the concept involves "the whole problem of human thought and of the objects of human thinking," [22] the "concept of law" is the central notion in any discipline concerned with knowledge of positive laws. It varies from legal philosophy to legal philosophy, and it is constructed with a view to maximizing understanding of law. By like token, therefore, the test of any concept of law involves the validity and significance of the supporting philosophy of law.

Concepts of Positive Law

In defining "positive law," one does not start with a *tabula rasa*. Instead, one finds the word "law" in his language and learns its uses in everyday speech. In some parts of the United States a policeman is "the law," and the cry, "The law is coming," is immediately understood by the participants in a game of dice. Then, if one is a careful reader of newspaper reports or becomes experienced in a business or, especially, if one studies law, he learns how lawyers use that term with reference to certain "authoritative materials" and, finally, he may read philosophy, social science, and the directly relevant jurisprudence and sociology of law and learn there are still other uses of the term. This progress is not a merely verbal one, for at every stage one observes what goes on, noting, for example, that law is concerned with the maintenance of order, the prevention and termination of conflicts, and so on. The uses of the word thus reflect knowledge of the relevant realities.

The presupposition of criticism of any concept of law is that there are better and worse concepts of law. And while the choice of a particular concept of law is partly a matter of individual preference, once a choice has been made, reflecting a certain purpose or interest, various conditions are encountered: the need to communicate, an existing language, the nature of relevant data, and so on. Accordingly, while legal philosophers and scientists sometimes take into account ordinary speech and the ways in which lawyers use the term "law," their final decision is largely determined by their purpose and the relevant data. Thus, "the concept of law" raises problems which may be solved in various ways, and any solution can be rather objectively appraised.

More particularly, "the concept of law" has meant defining "law" in terms of a writer's preference, an idea of law, that is, a mental construct, a universal, that is, the nature of the subject matter, and, recently, ordinary usage. In presenting these views of the "concept of law," legal philosophies reflect the principal positions taken vis à vis a perennial epistemological problem.

For example, Kelsen first states that "any attempt to define a concept must take for its starting-point the common usage of the word. . . ." He asks, next, whether "the social phenomena generally called 'law' present a common characteristic distinguishing them from all other social phenomena of a similar kind?" But he quickly decides that "the only question [regarding the concept of law] is whether they [our terms] will serve the theoretical purpose for which we have intended them." His "scientific reason" immediately leads Kelsen to ignore popular usage, especially whether that concept implies the moral validity of law, since his theoretical purpose requires him to dismiss that as "ideology." Later, he also excludes all factual connotations from his concept of law except the minimal references to fact necessary to make concepts intelligible. He argues, for example, that there is nothing in the intentional killing of a human being which makes that murder (he ignores social norms, the harm, and the social reaction); instead, he holds that concepts of penal law give that meaning to the otherwise meaningless facts. It becomes evident that Kelsen has very definite ideas about a "science of law" and that his theory of the legal concept is the "mixed" one known as conceptualism. For neither does he derive his concepts from conduct or any other external reality nor, despite occasional nominalist statements ("We may define at will those terms which we wish to use as tools in our intellectual work") does he construct merely verbal formulations.[23] Kelsen's concept of law should therefore be distinguished from those concepts related to nominalism and realism.[24]

John Austin, one of the founders of modern conceptualist

jurisprudence, also contemplated a juridical science relevant to the practice of law. In that perspective, the concept of law was defined by Austin in terms of "command of the Sovereign" and by Kelsen in terms of a "hypothetical judgment" specifying delict and sanction, and derived from a basic norm, thus avoiding the psychological connotations of "command." Despite Austin's vocabulary, however, it is possible to interpret his theory in terms of the implications of his ideas and thus recognize that many of his critics have gratuitously emphasized empirical difficulties concerning the "Sovereign." [25]

Legal Sanction

While the concept of law developed by Austin and Kelsen is dominant in many places, other concepts of law serve various purposes and disciplines. There is, however, a very wide agreement that the sanction is essential in any concept of law. To challenge the consensus in this regard of many otherwise divergent theories, whose exponents include St. Thomas Aquinas, Austin, Weber, Kelsen, and Cohen, would seem to be a rather formidable undertaking.[26]

Such a challenge was raised by Petrazhitsky and, possibly, by Ehrlich. Ehrlich sometimes seems to argue that sanction is not an essential part of positive law. He relies heavily on the fact that "in a considerable part of public law . . . and administrative law there is no compulsion . . . whatever." Cabinet ministers and parliamentary officials, he notes, cannot be coerced in the usual legal sense. He refers to international law, ecclesiastical law, and "almost all precepts regulating the competence and order of business of parliamentary bodies," as well as to rules concerning family and corporate relationships, as instances of positive laws which lack sanctions. Hence, he concludes, "legal compulsion" is "not an essential element of the concept of law." [27] For him, the "living law" was wholly a matter of conformity; and that is perhaps the principal, if not the always expressed, ground of the criticism that he confused positive law with custom. But Ehrlich's position is rather more complicated. He points out that legal norms, like all social norms, are sanctioned by public opinion, popular resentment and the like. Consistently, in his argument that legal norms are not necessarily "sanctioned," he refers to the usual specification of the legal sanction, namely, "threat of penalty or of compulsory execution." In sum, even in Ehrlich's sociology of law, the principal relevant problem is not whether law is sanctioned, but whether the legal sanction is distinctive.[28]

Petrazhitsky developed a psychological concept of law based on introspection, in which he distinguished among moral attitudes ("impulsions") those which are bilateral, attributing a right to one person and imposing a duty upon another ("positive law"), from impulsions which are not bilateral; for example, in charity, duties are imposed upon potential donors but rights are not attributed to the needy.[29] Apart from the questionable validity of this distinction, it is noteworthy that Petrazhitsky was very little concerned with the sociology of law. When he criticized the inclusion of the sanction in traditional concepts of law, he did so in terms of his psychology and the logic of infinite regression. But the fact that supreme court judges, for instance, are not subject to legal sanctions, if that be assumed, does not imply that the sanction is not "essential" in the concept of positive law or that the omission of the sanction improves analysis. It may mean that supreme court judges are not subject to legal control.

In a recent book, which restates Petrazhitsky's and Ehrlich's views regarding wills, contracts, and the like, Professor H. L. A. Hart also contends that positive law is not necessarily coercive. He argues that Austin and Kelsen erroneously adopted the model of criminal law as that of all law, whereas, he insists, most rules of law are "very unlike" criminal law.[30] By employing ordinary uses of the words "law" and "rules of law," [31] and relying also on what is "conceivable" as law,[32] he sought "to provide . . . a better understanding of the resemblances and differences between law, coercion, and morality, as types of social phenomena." [33]

Criticism of Austin's and Kelsen's concentration on the sanction is, of course, compatible with theories of legal sociology and natural law philosophy which find much more in law than its coerciveness.[34] But Professor Hart goes far beyond such criticism of this phase of legal positivism, arguing that it is misleading to include the sanction in the concept of law. Espousing ordinary usage and what is "conceivable," he finds that many "rules of law" concerning the making of contracts, wills, marriages, and so on are not sanctioned. Instead, such rules provide "facilities" —"a feature of law obscured by representing all law" as coercive.[35]

Obviously, one is free to make or forego making contracts, wills, and so on, and, on the other hand, everyone who commits a crime is subject to a sanction. But the elaboration of this in terms of ordinary meanings of "law" will hardly suffice in jurisprudence.[36]

In appraising the validity of the above thesis, one should ask (and it requires a very persistent effort *not* to ask): (a) what is the difference between a legal privilege (liberty) or legal power and a nonlegal one? and (b) are the privileges of making contracts, wills, and so on among the privileges protected by tort and criminal law? If these questions are asked, one directly confronts the fact that *legal* privileges and *legal* powers cannot be understood unless they are juxtaposed to illegal interference with them. Thus, it does not suffice simply to note that "the law" grants privileges and powers to many persons who decide whether they wish to use them. What is granted to them takes its meaning by reference to what "must" be done to persons who illegally interfere with the exercise of these privileges and to persons who become subject to legal sanctions partly because someone used a legal power.[37] To ignore this conveys the erroneous impression that all privileges and powers have the same meaning.

There are legal privileges (liberties) of walking on roads free from assault, engaging in trade free from depredation, making contracts and wills, getting married, expressing opinions, and so on, free from interference; indeed, all the privileges expressed in civil law take their distinctive meaning, in part, from their relation to the duties of tort and criminal law imposed on all potential violators of those liberties. As Kelsen put it, "Law is imperative for the one, and thereby permissive for the other." Moreover, even in ordinary discussion, it would be taking a very narrow view of criminal law to concentrate wholly on the duties and the sanctions and to ignore the basic liberties which the criminal law assures everybody.

The significance of the above-indicated relationships is not altered by the fact that the criminal law may be said to impose duties on "everybody," while many civil sanctions threaten only those who exercise their legal privileges and powers or various other persons affected by that exercise. Tort law, legally required "contracts," and a vast modern structure of social legislation directly controvert that view; but, apart from that, it is misleading to formulate the differences among various branches of law in those terms. For although some harms are so serious that they are forbidden by penal, tort, and other law (that is, duties are imposed on everybody in those regards), it is inapt to compare this with the fact that people are free as regards making contracts, just as it would be problematic to compare the making or the omission of making contracts with penal harms. Cogent comparisons are made among (a) privileges (liberties) to walk on streets, express opinions, engage in trade, make wills and contracts, (b) capacities to make contracts, wills, and so on, (c) interferences with the exercise of privileges and powers, (d) the respective duties after people have made contracts and the duties imposed by criminal law, (e) violations of the duties of civil and penal law, and (f) civil and penal sanctions.

In a democratic society, the community has for good reason placed itself (that is, everybody) under criminal, tort, and other duties. In most contracts, duty and subjection to civil sanctions depend, in part, on individual choice. But the inclusion of the sanction in concepts of law does not obscure this or any other important difference; on the contrary, as noted, it clarifies the meaning of legal privileges and legal powers. Nor does the specification that every violation of law (delict) must incur a sanction imply that law is wholly coercive or that legal privileges (liberties) are unimportant. "Liberty under law" combines the essential notions, and by common law, no one subjects himself to a criminal sanction unless he chooses to commit a proscribed harm; one is just as free to keep from violating a criminal law as he is to refrain from making and violating a contract.

So, too, the assertion that the various functions of rules or branches of law are obscured by specifying that the sanction is essential is not supported by isolating privileges and powers from the duties imposed on others not to violate those "facilities." Besides, the fact that rules of law are alike in being sanctioned does not alter the distinctiveness of the functions, say, of contract and criminal law; nor, on the other hand, does the fact that tort and penal duties are imposed on everyone imply that there are no differences in the functions of these branches of law. Coercion can be employed for many reasons; it can implement very different functions.

Kelsen's theory is vulnerable on various grounds in addition to its inadequacy for legal sociology resulting from its neglect of conformity and its distortion of the values implicit in delict and sanction.[38] But it is hardly an advance in legal theory to ignore Kelsen's purpose and charge him with the error of holding that law consists of directions to officials to impose sanctions.[39] On the first page of his principal work, Kelsen writes: "Every rule of law obligates human beings to observe a certain behavior under certain circumstances," [40] and this is repeated and made quite clear. The above criticism reveals a failure to grasp the significance of Kelsen's distinction between the "secondary norm," which is addressed to the subject, and the "primary norm," which specifies the sanction; [41] and it also overlooks the fact that the policies of addressing statutes to the public and of ordinary speech differ from the principal requirement of both analytical legal science and the sociology of law—to discover a concept of law in terms of significant uniformities. So, too, unless one recognizes the distinction Kelsen draws between the "rule of law," a term in his science of law, and the norms "created by the law-making authorities," his purpose is merely ignored.[42]

Kelsen carried his concept of law to the point of making the sanction the fulcrum of the theory, characterizing the delict solely by the fact that a sanction must be imposed for its occurrence. In his theory, "harm" means *only* a condition for imposition of a sanction. Take away the sanction, and his entire system collapses. But the limitation in this respect is not Kelsen's insistence on the coerciveness of law—for here he only joins the vastly preponderant view—but that by holding values, especially justice, to be irrational, ideological, and so on, he can find no disvalue in any delict. Law, therefore, becomes sheer force, unqualified by reason or desert. It is this aspect of Kelsen's theory which also accounts for its inadequacy with regard to conformity to law [43] and which, for various other reasons, casts doubt upon its claim to be a "general" theory of law.

Austin and Kelsen were obviously familiar with legal concepts [44] and ordinary usage. To criticize them on the premise that they were simply seeking "an advance in clarity" [45] and that "law" should be "equally if not more concerned with the 'puzzled man' or 'ignorant man'" is to misconceive the principal intent of legal positivism—a juridical science. Its authors distinguished parts of a rule of law from a rule of law, and they restated declaratory forms of constitutional and statutory provisions to conform to the normative-imperative structure of a congruent concept of law. Accordingly, given the purpose to construct a concept of law "from the standpoint of science," [46] it is merely irrelevant that ordinary usage often takes a different direction and that constitutional and statutory provisions do not always include sanctions. The pertinent jurisprudential issues regarding "the concept of law" are not met until one asks why Austin and Kelsen included the sanction in their concept of law. Plainly, they thought it necessary to distinguish positive law from other norms; this could not be done unless the sanction was considered part of the concept of positive law.[47] This does not imply that positive law should be distinguished only by reference to the sanction because, except in legal positivism, the sanction bears a rational relationship to the quality of the delict and is, in part, determined by that relationship. Nor does it imply that the inclusion of the sanction renders it easy, in the sociology of law, to distinguish positive law from the rules of fashion, mores, and ethics.

Natural law philosophers have insisted on the sanction in positive law because justice requires that wrongdoing be met by the imposition of an apt privation. In other terms, one reason why positive law is morally valid is that it provides due sanctions. Legal sociologists, excepting rare dissenters, have included the sanction in their concept of positive law not only because that provides an essential criterion by reference to which law can be substantively distinguished from other types of social control but also because the imposition of legal sanctions is very important in other respects, for example, in the maintenance of the community's values or attitudes.[48] Thus, while Durkheim and Weber disagreed on various issues, both made coerciveness essential in positive law, the latter holding that a corps of enforcement officials is the most important of all the criteria by which positive law is distinguished from nonlegal norms. The paramount consideration is that each component of the legal structure, taken alone, dissolves in an ocean of like data. The inclusion of the sanction is required to construct a totality (positive law) regarding which distinctive questions of ethics and social science may be raised.

Certainly, no legal scholar would disparage the elucidation of ordinary meanings of words, including "law" and "rule of law," and it is also necessary to defend common sense against an authoritarian *expertise* claiming a superior knowledge of daily life. But while it is important to preserve and improve common understanding, solution of the major problems confronting legal philosophers requires much more than that.[49] The failure to provide any concept or "definition" of law implies that no theoretical basis has been laid for the construction of any discipline designed to increase knowledge of law. The principal, extremely difficult problem currently facing legal comparatists and others interested in relevant social studies is to construct a concept of law which facilitates the acquisition of social knowledge of law; and neither ordinary nor positivist concepts of law suffice for that purpose.

Positive Law and Jurisprudence

Positive law is the subject matter of jurisprudence; the concepts of jurisprudence are "about" the concepts of positive law. Conversely, "concept of law" is not a term of positive law, nor are right-duty, power-liability, privilege, and so on. They are concepts of jurisprudence. Similarly, as regards comparative law, that is, humanistic sociology of law, the above relationship also obtains—positive laws, in a congruent sense, are the subject matter, and the sociology of law is knowledge of that subject matter.

There is, of course, a close interplay between the concepts of positive laws and the knowledge of them expressed in jurisprudence and other disciplines. If we compare primitive law with advanced legal systems, we find not merely a far greater number of rules in the latter but also the reflection of a vast increase in knowledge of law shown in the organization of codes into general and special parts, classification into branches such as tort and contract, criminal, property, family, succession, public and procedural law, as well as structures like "trust" and "corporation." The concepts of positive law range from the specificity of legislative divorces, judicial judgments and decrees naming particular persons, to the generality of principles of positive law taken as norms applied by the courts, for example, that there must be an act to incur criminal liability and, thence, to such wider constructions as those noted first above.

Rules of law refer to acts, events, and other facts; the logical manipulation of the interrelations of the rules and principles reveals many other meanings implied in the formal side of law, which Beale emphasized.[50] Every rule of law can be analyzed in terms of the elements comprising it, each of which is also a compound concept. For example, in burglary, "breaking" is distinguished from "entry," and so on, and those "material" concepts rest finally upon elementary acts of recognition of the qualia of experience and comparison. The common law definition of burglary takes its meaning in one direction from its place in the penal code among a certain class of crimes. In the other direction, it is defined in terms of its five "material" elements, each of which is a simpler concept that includes more elementary uniformities. Thus, concepts of positive law specify certain similar aspects of legally relevant actions and things: "entering" may be done in many ways by many means, and each entry, even if made through the same window, is always different in some way from every other entry. The concept is in terms of the sameness of all entries.

Since positive laws are the subject matter of jurisprudence and this subject matter includes references to certain facts and qualities, so, too, though less directly, do the concepts comprising jurisprudence. The utility and also the limitations of the concepts of jurisprudence result from the high level of their generalization. For example, the concepts of law, right-duty, power-liability, and so on refer to relations expressed in all the rules of all legal systems. Their function is to communicate "essential" meanings in such high abstraction as to fit all the legal relations implied in all the (formally defined) laws of all systems. An analogue of their function is provided by the basic concepts of physics where, in terms of mass, matter, energy, friction, inertia, velocity, and so on, physicists generalize about the movements of all the material bodies in the universe. So, too, the elementary notions of conceptual jurisprudence, now explicated chiefly in legal positivism, subsume many thousands of rules and millions of transactions. In adjudication, they culminate in a single concept—the right-duty relation—and when that has been rendered determinate with reference to particular parties, the mandate of the court is specified in terms which legal sanctions implement. The "concept of law" represents the maximum generalization among those universal ideas. From rules of law, right-duty, power-liability, and so on, one ascends to the ultimate jurisprudential notion which all the others presuppose—the concept of law.

Common Concepts of Comparative Law

While conceptualist comparative law must be distinguished from the more general knowledge of law characteristic of analytical jurisprudence, both have the same subject matter, namely, concepts of positive law. The "common concept" of the legal comparatist is, therefore, neither a concept of positive law, as Gutteridge observed, nor, on the other hand, since it is limited to a few legal systems, is it a high-level abstraction such as the concept of law, the right-duty relation, and so on.

The legal comparatist is familiar with the concepts of positive law of his "system" and he compares them with other positive laws. His purpose is to discover common concepts among these concepts of positive law. Theoretically, if two or more positive laws are identical, the common concept coincides with them. But even then, the common concept has an independent status in comparative law since it represents the uniformity of positive laws. That uniformity, as stated, subsists in the very laws themselves—it is not something external, imposed on them. Its status and character become clearer when the legal comparatist describes the differences among the positive laws compared. The mind lifts the similarity of certain rules or parts of them from its subject matter as it constructs the common concept of the comparative discipline. In closely related legal systems, that is, where one was transplanted or imitated or where both have a common origin, rules may be phrased in similar or even identical terms, and their meanings may also be very similar. But even in this situation and, plainly, in systems not so closely connected, the common concept is distinguishable from those rules. Sometimes, for instance, as regards the trust, the common concept in American and Continental law is found among aggregates of rules of law. The common concept connotes the similarities. It defines a class.

I have been discussing the common concept derived by legal scholars in comparison of a limited number of laws. It is a type of comparison that requires only two items, although there may be more than that. In any case, the question is, what is common among the members of this class? A different kind of comparison and a different concept are involved when at least three items are compared with each other in terms of degree (A resembles C more than it does B). In this type of comparison, laws or other data can be arranged in a series. The wider implications of this type of comparison will be discussed later.[51]

As stated, the sociological legal comparatist, having discovered his common quarry, proceeds—in historical narrative and on a level of generalization limited to a few items—to describe and explain it. He contributes his distinctive knowledge in terms of cultural legal history, comparison of leading case-histories, description (especially of the differences in positive laws, their functions, and trends), and correlations found among laws of a few countries. In this role of a humanist in legal sociology, many other concepts and theories, drawn from the social disciplines, are required; some of the principal ones will be considered later.

When the legal comparatist proceeds from the study of legislation and case law to that of the treatise, he brings the concepts of positive law within the orbit of theories of law. This work is further enlightened, not merely safeguarded from error, by consultation with lawyers experienced in the system foreign to the comparatist.[52] The nuances differentiating concepts of positive law are sometimes so nice that it is only in conversation with representative scholars that the particular nub of a problem is revealed and an insight into the common features is secured. The comparative study of rules of law may go further and take account of relevant procedures, the practices of courts, officials, and lawyers, and of the style employed in analyzing legal problems, for these may have important effects on the substantive law. Thus the seemingly diverse tasks allocated to conceptualist comparative law (*droit comparé dogmatique*) find rational places in a general theory through their relation to the common concept derived from the variety of data indicated above.[53] This common concept is evidently different from, and more significant than, the relatively formal concepts derived solely from the authoritative materials.

In this work, comparative scholars accept the axiom that one learns something new by having it assimilated to what is already familiar.[54] Foreign law is thus explained by assimilating knowledge of it to the comparatist's knowledge of his national law.[55] This comparative study is eminently sound as far as it goes. But it does not go far enough.

If, for example, a German scholar compares certain rules of French and German contract law to the above extent, what are the legal scholars of other systems to make of that study? [56] If the readers were assumed to be German-trained lawyers, the natural omission of discussion on German law will make the report difficult reading for lawyers not versed in that law. Valuable as are his services in stating his results in terms which are intelligible to his fellow lawyers who are not familiar with the foreign law, so long as the research terminates in the translation of foreign laws in terms of resemblance to and difference from the domestic ones, the range of its significance remains a limited one. Even for the German-trained lawyers, the potentialities of comparative study have only been touched.

An important step beyond that can be taken by formulating common concepts to include the similarities among the foreign and the domestic rules. The relevant knowledge is, indeed, already implied in the preceding step and the customary report. But more than a different emphasis is involved in the articulation of the common concept, and especially in the report of it in terms that are understood by readers other than the comparatist's national lawyers. For example, one's national law would need to be described, and the ways in which the respective rules are classified in the compared systems would need to be explained.[57] If the potentialities of this method are still further developed, it may be possible to discover a theory which subsumes what is common in entire branches of all legal systems. This is *rapprochement* advanced to the level of what may be called "transnational theory." [58] The terms of a transnational theory may be formally identical with those used in the theories of the national systems compared, but their meaning will differ.

This can be illustrated by summarizing a transnational theory of criminal law.[59] This theory is stated in terms which subsume most of what is generally recognized as penal law in all advanced systems, excepting negligent damage and other nonvoluntary offenses. The theory distinguishes the propositions comprising the penal law as rules, doctrines,[60] and principles. Rules specify the distinctive characteristics of the various crimes and they also include such terms as "any person," "kills," "burns" and so on. Doctrines are intermediate propositions which concern infancy, insanity, intoxication, mistake of fact or law, coercion, necessity, and attempt, solicitation and conspiracy; and the principles, the widest concepts, are seven in number and concern *mens rea*, act (manifested effort), the concurrence or fusion of *mens rea* and act to form conduct, harm, causation (connecting conduct and harm), the punitive sanction, and, finally, legality.[61]

The definitions of the crimes are stated in terms of the rules qualified by all the doctrines; and the necessity of doing this is apparent from the fact, for example, that an infant or an insane person who does what is forbidden in the rules does not commit a crime. The principles are defined, first, as abstractions from the combined totality of the rules and doctrines and, second, by reference to their teleological interrelations. Thus, the principle of *mens rea* is abstracted from the common character of all the specific *mentes reae*, qualified by all the relevant doctrines: insanity, infancy, mistake, and so on. The principle of punishment abstracts what is common to all the sanctions, and so on as to the other principles. Second, in terms of this theory, criminal conduct bears a teleological relation to harm, which, in its turn, derives its meaning, in part, as the end brought about by the criminal conduct. Causation is also given a congruent meaning, that is, it is limited to the kind of causation manifested in end-seeking; but this does not exclude the relevance of physical causality, since human actors are subject to that and must take account of it when they commit penal harms. Finally, the punitive sanction is also rationally related to the harm and thus to the relevant conduct.

The theory is thus descriptive of a unitary field comprised of voluntary harm-doing within the limits of penal law. In its terms, there are no "formal crimes" or "crimes" resulting from accident or inadvertence. Finally, and especially pertinent, is that the theory purports to be universal in the sense of fitting the most significant parts of all systems of penal law, namely, those characterized by voluntary harm-doing. In sum, a set of concepts which meet the specifications of certain principles was formulated to subsume the principal part of the penal law of all legal systems and all other crimes proscribed there which conform to the principles.

Just as a scientist must have in mind an hypothesis in order to engage in meaningful research, so, too, comparative lawyers start with a theory of their national law. This becomes an hypothesis with reference to other legal systems, and the study of foreign law tests the possibility of extending the theory of the national law to include the foreign law. Thus, conceptualist comparative law proceeds from the translation of foreign concepts in terms of one's own law to the formulation of common concepts and thence to transnational theory, the systematization of this knowledge. Transnational theory may be viewed as the ultimate reach of comparative law or, if one prefers, as a bridge from that to legal science. For transnational theory at most subsumes only a branch of all legal systems, and its concepts are relatively close to those of the positive law, for example, in the above theory, the distinctiveness of penal law is preserved. It therefore falls short of the high level of abstraction of analytical jurisprudence which subsumes all positive law in terms of ultimate conceptions —the idea of law, right-duty, and so on.

The above discussion of transnational theory shows the place and function of legal principles as the basic organizational constructs of legal theories. For, as was indicated in the above summary of a theory of criminal law, principles subsume a myriad of rules and doctrines. But in the process of abstraction in which principles are derived, one ignores the distinctiveness of the rules and doctrines. Perhaps this is what elicited Gutteridge's remark that "rules which are avowedly universal in character do not lend themselves to comparison." [62] This is apt if only principles are compared, hence the criticism must be construed as a caveat to communicate the detail of the rules and doctrines from which the principles were derived.[63]

The need to do this can be illustrated with reference to the principle of legality in criminal law, *nulla poena sine lege*, which is sometimes said to be common to all modern legal systems. Some systems, however, include rules which define criminal conduct very broadly, and if that is not reported, statements about a "common" principle of legality are misleading. Moreover, when the application of *nulla poena* to particular cases is observed in different countries, it becomes clear that the principle actually has many different meanings; indeed, there must be some differences in any two systems. In some countries, there is such a paucity of case-law and treatises that judicial interpretation is much freer than in countries where a veritable mountain of precedent and a large professional literature must be consulted. And, evidently, if the executive controls judicial decision or if he requires secret trials for political offenders, it is very misleading to say that that system includes "the" principle of legality.

Even within a class of very similar systems, to say, for instance, that the principle of fault is common to Western penal law would also have dubious significance. For "fault" has substantially different meanings in these legal systems, for example, as regards ordinary (unconscious) negligence. Legal systems also contain official "escape clauses" from the rigor of legality by providing that there was "fault" if the defendant "could have" known the relevant facts or "could have" acted properly, and the subjective opinion of the judge concerning "fault" is decisive. This implies that any realistic comparison of principles must also take account of official practices which affect the determination of the substantive law.

The difficulties met in trying to discover legal principles and to derive their meaning from the factual and valuational meanings of the sustaining lesser norms, relevant practices, and whatever else is influential should not obscure the fact that knowledge of the principles is extremely valuable. We do not understand a body of law or its resemblance to branches of other systems until we have pushed inquiry to the point of discovering their common underlying principles. If the principles are first elucidated in the context of the respective rules and doctrines from which they are abstracted, and so on, a comparison of their consequent actual meanings is highly significant, as is implied to some extent in the wide consensus that a rule of law cannot be thoroughly understood in isolation from the system to which it belongs.

The fact that the meaning of legal rules is determined by their relation to "relevant realities" raises difficult questions in view of sharp cultural differences which determine the meaning of words. At what point is a "contract" not really a contract? [64] There are many "bills of rights" stated in identical terms. But they differ widely in meaning when the formulas are defined by reference to relevant realities, including the procedural implementation that is readily available and effective in some countries.[65]

Again, some penal codes specify the same punishment for criminal attempt and for the relevant consummated crime; and a study terminated at that point would leave the impression that there is a great difference between that law and the law in other countries. But a study of the sentences actually imposed upon attemptors may show that what happens is very much alike in those systems. A law phrased in terms of strict penal liability is a different concept from one which requires negligence to convict. But if the enforcement of the former law is restricted to cases where there was at least negligence, do the actual concepts differ? That "comparability" involves factual and valuational questions was previously indicated in the interpretation of "comparative law" as humanistic legal sociology; this phase of the problem will be more fully discussed in the next chapter.

We have been leading conceptualist comparative law in the direction of the sociology of law, but before proceeding further in that direction we must pause and weigh certain pertinent issues. One need not be a Platonist to believe that ideas are very tough things which have a life of their own, preserving a hard core of meaning despite changing social contexts. Consider the age of the ideas of possession, crime, liability, right-duty, and many others. No doubt, Austin stood on firm ground in his appreciation of legal concepts. Nor is it a mere coincidence that Lambert emphasized *rapprochement*, as did Bryce's and Beale's "system," and that, despite the appeal of the theory that comparative law is a kind of social science and despite proposals to study the "function" and "social context" of laws, most comparatists continue in the classical path of seeking and elucidating common ideas.

From the vantage point of this tradition, even the injunction to delineate the social context of rules may seem dubious counsel. Suppose one wished to compare the English, French, and German rules on criminal "negligence." Would the knowledge of the respective social contexts be helpful? Could a more realistic knowledge of the similarities and differences among the laws of the Scandinavian countries regarding the respective rights of innocent purchasers and owners be acquired by studying the social contexts in which the various rules function? [66] Could the respective social contexts be differentiated sufficiently, for example, to account for the differences in the laws of criminal attempt or burglary and Continental counterparts, or in the laws concerning undisclosed agency? [67]

The issue cuts deeper than that of relevancy, setting ideas *against* social factors. For what is sometimes insinuated in theories of "social context" is that economic, political, and other cultural forces determine the law, so that even if social context is expanded to include philosophical and social thought, that is viewed as a merely ideological influence on a par with economic factors. This is another reason why comparative law can never be reduced to a sociology comprised only of descriptive causal generalizations. For comparative law holds fast to the distinctiveness, autonomy, and value of legal ideas.

In 1900 Lambert argued that there should be complete separation between comparative law viewed as legal sociology and that much older conceptualist comparative law which sought the *rapprochement* of laws, *droit commun législatif*. Lambert thought that in teaching, it would be dangerous to consolidate the two sciences of comparative law, whose spirit and role, he said, differed profoundly.[68] He even argued that the comparative law whose object was the discovery of common concepts should be rid of its tie to the sociology of law which had, in his vivid phrase, "paralyzed its flight."[69] The following question therefore arises: Are there two separate, autonomous disciplines of comparative law—the one comprising a type of social knowledge while the other, conceptualist comparative law, pursuing an entirely independent path, lays bare the concepts common to various legal systems?

Lambert himself gave the clue to the answer when he later wrote that "comparative jurisprudence and law as a social science are two aspects of the same thing."[70] His earlier appraisal had been influenced by Comte's sociology, which almost completely ignored positive law and was hostile to its conceptual character. Since then, the rise of a normative sociology influenced by the work of Dilthey, Durkheim, and Weber, qualified, however, by theories of values, especially those of Dewey, Hartmann, Ross, and Ewing, have revealed the compatibility of norms with the facts of social action. Present solutions are, therefore, no longer confined to a hard choice between conceptualism and positivist sociology. In the light of the humanistic normative social science that can be brought to bear on the incidence of the codes, statutes, and case law in social action, there must be a tentativeness about the meaning of legal concepts derived only from the authoritative materials of positive law and the legal treatises. Indeed, much more than that is involved in the construction of a humanistic legal sociology, as will be seen in the following chapter.

Conceptualist analysis limited to the authoritative materials is, no doubt, very important, and many scholars may be content to remain within those limits in discharging that arduous task. Most comparatists would agree that in many instances it is necessary to study, in addition, relevant official practices and special modes of analyzing legal problems. But what is wanted, finally, is knowledge of what actually happens in society, as well as among the State's officials, not only for practical reasons but also because the acquisition of the maximum knowledge of law is desired.[71] Conceptualist study, limited to the authoritative materials and legal treatises and even enlightened by the study of official practices, styles, and techniques, can at best provide a fraction of the relevant knowledge of law, determined largely by the prevailing standards of adjudication. Only study that is not restricted by practical objectives or exigencies can supply the full ambit of knowledge of the relevant social realities. This is surely the province of comparative study concerned with the social context and function of laws.

We have explored the implications of these references of legal comparatists as well as the sociological theory of the 1900 Congress, which is still very much alive today if, indeed, it is not dominant among social scientists; and this led to the conclusion that "comparative law" is the intermediate social knowledge discussed above, that is, humanistic legal sociology. We must now supplement the preliminary statement of this theory since it can hardly be assumed that legal concepts are the subject matter of this discipline even though it may be inferred from the above discussion that they must be given an important place in that subject matter.

4

THE SOCIAL REALITY
OF LAW

The most sustained work in the history of jurisprudence has been devoted to theories of positive law. Far from being futile or superfluous, such efforts are the surest sign that legal scholars are attending to fundamental problems and are, also, contributing to "general" philosophy.[1] Certainly, the principal difficulty which has hindered the progress of "comparative law" and other social disciplines concerned with law has been, and is, uncertainty regarding their subject matter. There have, to be sure, been suggestive references by legal comparatists to function, problem-solving, institution, and so on. But this has not been followed by inquiries regarding the implications of these references for a congruent theory of positive law; and the current statement that "comparative law" is "the comparative method" applied to the study of "positive law" is little more than a formality.

When it is said that legal comparatists study positive laws, when statements are made about a science of law or a humanistic sociology of law, when anthropologists study primitive law, and political scientists state that their common interest is in "legal government," what is the meaning or what are the meanings of the word thus employed to refer to the subject matter of these disciplines? And if one agrees that the social context of laws is very important, he must also determine what that social context is and how it is related to law.

The effect of various philosophies and epistemologies on the construction of concepts of law was discussed in the preceding chapter. But from a more immediate point of view, two significant lines of organization are discernible in the labyrinth of definitions of positive law. The first is that certain important social purposes have been very influential; and second, the jurisprudential and other knowledge constructed on these definitions is either practical or theoretical knowledge. The first insight directly concerns positive law; the second, the knowledge of it. Evidently, both are very closely interconnected, indeed, they are aspects of a jurisprudence which integrates large parts of legal philosophies that even now are usually assumed to be irreconcilable.

Three Perspectives in Defining "Positive Law"

Disputes about the nature of positive law did not originate in the *Weltanschauung* of a philosopher or in theories of the "concept" or "universal." They had their origin in very important practical problems which human beings have had to face throughout history; it is this experience and the words used to discuss these problems that we must try to understand.

The oldest of these problems, as reported in Western classics, is that of justice, especially in the relation of citizens to their rulers. When one follows the ramifications of the relevant polemics as they unfold in the Platonic Dialogues,[2] in discussions of consent and natural rights, and in reports of experience of twentieth-century dictatorship, the question which transcends all others is that of the obligation of civic obedience. The position taken by those who thought that was a very serious problem was as simple as might be imagined—the obligation did not extend to the ruler's immoral commands.

This problem was, of course, discussed in the words of particular languages laden with traditional usages. The earliest connotations of "law" were religious ones, for example, the "laws of God"; and the word had consequently acquired an honorific meaning. That is why Socrates, when the Thirty Tyrants commanded him to arrest Leon of Salamis, refused to obey, not the law, but the "order" of these rulers. Ordinary speech, or at least that part of it which appealed to Socrates when he faced this problem, apparently suggested that "law" be withheld from the Sovereign's unjust commands. When contemporary philosophers assert that this age-old controversy is "merely verbal" they are, in effect, complaining about, but hardly altering, the conditions of communication. Certainly, the problems of justice, including that of the relations of citizens and government, remain very much alive; [3] and in democratic societies questions are constantly raised in terms which reflect the Socratic distinction even if the ordinary meaning of "law" does not observe it.

In dealing with this problem, one is not required to perpetuate the language habits of bygone ages; and the present writer is among those who think "natural law" is an unfortunate term, confusing physical nature with ethical principles and the rational appeal of values with the coerciveness of positive law. Still, it remains a very important fact that positive law has for centuries been defined in certain terms by men facing their most important civic problem—a practical problem requiring that unjust commands, or "laws," if one prefers, be distinguished from just ones. Whatever linguistic preferences one may have, the practical problems persist, not least in the unceasing search for "right law" in adjudication. The practical perspective of natural law philosophy is thus a perennial one.

The knowledge acquired in this perspective directly concerns action, especially the goals which should be sought. On the other hand, when men seek to construct a legal science or a humanistic sociology of law, they are engaged in a theoretical inquiry. Practical inquiry, however, draws upon the theoretical knowledge, while what is done in practice becomes part of the subject matter of theoretical inquiry. The interrelations of these types of knowledge are complicated and cannot be discussed here. It must suffice to note that the conditions which determine the construction of the sciences and social disciplines differ importantly from those which influence the knowledge designed to solve practical problems.

The subject matter of any sociology of law cannot be all the commands of the Sovereign, good, bad, wise, stupid, obeyed, or ignored; and since the subject matter of a social discipline must be at least partly factual,[4] it cannot consist solely of concepts or rules, even though all of them are rational and just. It is possible, of course, for psychologists to study the behavior of rulers, including insane dictators and all their orders. But this would not contribute to sociology of law or of government in the sense of dealing with a uniform subject matter. To state these requirements of a social discipline in terms of the implications of empirical knowledge may suggest a Kantian bias, exemplified in Karl Pearson's theory. More apt is the theory suggested by Savigny, Durkheim, cultural anthropologists, and other social scientists, namely, that there are social norms which are discovered and operate spontaneously in the uncoerced solution of social problems. In order to distinguish these natural norms from commands and concepts, such words as "living law," "actual law," "law-in-action," "normative facts," and so on have been used.

The discovery of the uniform, substantive properties of positive law, or (if one prefers at this stage of the discussion) of this kind of positive law, is of the highest importance. It limits the subjective formulation of concepts of law and can also be made the basis for the construction of types of law and the classification of legal institutions. It implies a set of conditions which qualify hypotheses and generalizations about laws and government. In scientific generalization about falling bodies, the combination of chemical elements, the economic market, and so on, there is always a set of appended or implied conditions. Likewise, the knowledge comprised in the sociology of law and related disciplines can be valid only under certain conditions, and the most important condition is the restriction of "positive law" to the free solution of social problems. This implies that positive law, as a natural concomitant or product of the free solution of social problems, includes an "ideal element."

This obviously raises difficult questions in the social disciplines—about the long, diverse course and character of government in human affairs and, also, how this quality of law (or of certain "laws") may be employed in research. But without such a natural datum, jurisprudence is only a polemic of individual preferences; with it, it is anchored in actuality and becomes amenable to objective criticism. The pervasiveness and perdurance of customary law in all countries,[5] even under dictatorship, is sufficient to establish the cogency of the above postulate and, as indicated, there are other reasons to support it. The problem is complicated because theoretical and practical knowledge interact; for example, natural law philosophers have made use of the knowledge of what has been called "living law," "actual law," and so on. But they use it in criticism, to influence the correct solution of practical problems, while legal sociologists use it in describing the uniform subject matter of their discipline in conformity with the requirements of theoretical knowledge.

With reference to the terminology of the sociologies of law and related disciplines, it might be assumed that the thing to do is to speak of "actual positive law," "living law," "law-in-action," or the like, as sociological jurists have suggested. Certainly, the dominance of "the Sovereign's command" suggests that other words than "positive law" should be used to designate the social reality of law. On the merits of the question, however, and in a long-range view of it, this linguistic problem is not so easily solved. The bulking fact of customary law and the social and theoretical significance of spontaneously, rationally discovered norms which, after all, is what allows positive law in any sense to have abiding importance, might make it preferable for the legal sociologist to speak simply of "positive law" when he refers to his subject matter. The practice of law and ordinary speech may in some contexts be more important than theory, but this does not require the vocabulary of theorists to conform to that of practice or ordinary language. The legal sociologist can no more allow the practical and ordinary uses of "positive law" to determine his vocabulary than a physicist can permit engineering and daily speech to fix the terminology of physics. Admittedly, however, some concession is required in the light of traditional usage and the rudimentary character of socio-legal knowledge. Accordingly, when it seems necessary, I shall speak of "law-as-conduct" and "law as social reality" rather than simply of "positive law," and I shall distinguish the former from "merely" laws of the State.

In sum, the sociology of law is oriented to the solution of theoretical problems, while natural law philosophy, although it incorporates some of the theoretical knowledge, is oriented to action in the solution of practical problems, especially those involving political obligation and the search for "right law." Given that perspective and the honorific connotation of "law," the insistence of natural law philosophers that the term be restricted to the ruler's morally valid orders was normal speech, and it is also defensible on the above ground concerning the character of freely made or discovered law.

The third principal perspective which has influenced the definition of positive law is the practical one of the lawyer. There, the basic concern is with what the government may do to its subjects, the lawyer's clients. When this problem is faced by practitioners who appeal to the tribunals of the Sovereign and by scholars who, like Austin, construct a juridical science to meet the needs of lawyers, they must take as their province all the Sovereign's commands. For in that perspective, even the most arbitrary commands of the Sovereign may be the basis for imposing sanctions. Advocacy appeals to the Sovereign to stay his hand unless he has, in fact, ordered thus and so, that is, unless the instant case comes within the orbit of one of his commands. Facing the ruler hardly encourages arguments phrased in terms of "mere command" and another language habit is developed in this context. In more objective social terms, there is the need for certainty and regularity in the conduct of human affairs, including and necessitating the settlement of disputes. The ultimate premise in this practical perspective is therefore determined by the conditions of a legal state (*Rechtsstaat*)—here, authority must have the last word.[6] In other words, in practice, authority is just as "ultimate" as right is, and expression must be given to this fact in juridical science. This implies that there is some value in any body of law as opposed to utter chaos and, also, that that part of legal positivism which constitutes a juridical science congruent with the above perspective performs a necessary function; hence, it is the claim that legal positivism is an adequate or complete science and philosophy of law which raises difficulties.

In democratic states there are ways to challenge the validity of a Sovereign's command on the ground that it violates "the conditions of civilized living," and if the challenge is successful, the implication is that the command in issue is not a law. In the realm of practice there are, accordingly, areas of uncertainty and tension between the two practical positions. The natural law perspective, which supports authority as well as morality, tolerates compromises regarding doubtful issues, or the values of democratic society make orderly change preferable to civil disobedience. On the other hand, the practice of law, whether by judge or by lawyer, cannot be separated in normal conditions from the search for "right law." But these concessions do not alter the logic or distinctive character of each perspective or the unavoidable clash between rational authority and arbitrary command in the realm of practice. In the realm of theory, however, that is, in the sociology of law, different considerations obtain, for example, as regards the uniformity of the subject matter.

In conformity with his perspective, a legal positivist, as a juridical scientist, defines "positive law" in terms of certain minimal properties—in the form of a hypothetical proposition describing a delict and prescribing the imposition of a sanction; and he also specifies the fact of origin from the "Sovereign" or logical derivation from a postulated ultimate norm. He may acknowledge that other facts are important, for example, those regarding the "efficacy" of law, but he insists that they lie outside its essential character. A natural law philosopher accepts the formal definition of positive law as necessary, but not as sufficient. By requiring, in addition, that the command be morally valid, he narrows the class of law. Finally, in humanistic legal sociology, where value is also required on ontological grounds and for valid description, not criticism, of what law is in that perspective, the class of law is still further narrowed in one direction by the addition of the property of factuality, while it is enlarged in another, by eliminating the "political Sovereign," to include the laws of various subgroups which substantively accord with the specified criteria. In consequence of this diversity, difficulties are encountered in the literature of comparative law from the very beginning, and the failure to articulate the underlying perspective—the first requirement of comparability—obscures the fact that each of the representative concepts of law denotes a different subject matter. This also indicates the inevitable indeterminacy of discussions whether "in general" it is better to define "law" in positivist or in natural law terms.

Thus, the inadequacy of legal positivism for comparative study is simply an implication of the sociological perspective of such study. For example, while a moderate legal positivist like Austin made sense of the valuation of laws in terms of their utility, he allocated that function to "legislation"; that is, in his perspective it lay outside the scope of a jurisprudence which, also, was little concerned with facts. The inadequacy of legal positivism for comparative study becomes clearer by reference to Kelsen's view of justice and it becomes obvious in his explicit exclusion of the sociology of law ("comparative law") from the scope of the Pure Theory. Excluding the whole dimension of value and most of that of fact, legal positivism concentrates on universal forms —the concept of law, the right-duty relation, and the like.[7]

It is noteworthy, in this connection, that although Austin studied in Germany before taking up his work as the first professor of jurisprudence in the University of London, he did not acquire an interest in the comparative study of law. As Gutteridge observed, Austin "only makes a passing reference to comparative jurisprudence"; and Professor Brusiin adds, "In fact, the method he [Austin] has applied seems to exclude even the possibility of comparative research."[8] His interest, in conformity with his practical perspective, was in concepts common to all Sovereigns' commands, regardless of their rationality, operation, or effect. Accordingly, legal positivism neither required nor encouraged the study of the differences among laws which are inevitable concomitants of cultural similarities. Such "substantive" criteria are the *sine qua non* of comparative study.[9]

It does not follow that every empirically oriented theory of law is helpful in comparative study. For example, sociological positivism, including its Marxist version, conflicts with the premises of humanistic legal sociology regarding, for instance, the value of laws; and a meaningful description of functions, problem-solving, and so on cannot be given if valuation is treated as "ideology." Even more serious is the subordination of the legal "super-structure" to economic forces, which, in effect, eliminates legal ideas. For whatever philosophy "comparative law" reflects, it postulates the distinctiveness as well as the importance of legal ideas.

Law-as-Conduct

Since every social discipline has a subject matter that is partly factual, this must also be true of the sociology of law. This raises very difficult questions because, in conformity with that premise, the sociology of *law* implies that its subject matter consists not merely of facts which only "parallel" legal norms or of conduct "oriented" to them, but that law itself is, in part at least, factual. Viewed against the long history of legal philosophy, in which "law" has meant rules or concepts, this must raise very serious questions.

That history also shows, however, that for the past 150 years theories of positive law in factual terms have challenged the traditional concepts of law. What is involved, therefore, is not a marginal penchant but a widespread movement in legal thought which, dating from Savigny's perception of a "living law" as a kind of social reality, has continued to the present day in the quest of many scholars for a theory of law that takes due account of its actual character. Just as there are very important facts and problems which determine the practical perspectives of natural law philosophy and juridical science, so, too, are there important facts and problems which focus current social theory on the actuality of positive law. To an extent, this has always interested some scholars; Aristotle spoke of the constitution as "a way of life," and it has long been recognized that customary law is pervasive and potent, that the common law grew from traditional social practices, and so on. With the rise of the modern social sciences, the cultural character of positive law increasingly became the subject of study; and Savigny and Sir Henry Maine, a comparatist-legal sociologist, stood at the threshold of this movement.

In this century there have been many sustained efforts to provide a theory of positive law in empirical terms, and they have invariably met serious opposition, even from scholars sympathetic to that purpose. Chief among the difficulties has been, and is, the normativity of law. One cannot accept the reduction of that or other values to fact, for example, Petrazhitsky's impulsions, Duguit's intended *solidarité sociale*, the American Realists' official behavior, and the Scandinavian Realists' disinterested attitudes, even though the sensitivity of these scholars to the criteria of an adequate twentieth-century jurisprudence is apparent. The relevant lesson is that values and ideas, including the normativity of law, must be preserved as distinctive in the subject matter of the sociology of law. Some of the supporting foundations of this principle were laid by Plato and Aristotle, but the current jurisprudential theories are apt to be based on (1) normative social science built upon, even though in important ways it departs from, the sociology of Durkheim and Weber, (2) on phenomenology, and (3) on twentieth-century ethics, especially that of Dewey, Hartmann, Scheler Ross, and Ewing. The central insight of the relevant theories of law, which are being developed in various orientations by scholars in several countries, is that positive law is a distinctive type of *conduct*, a fusion of legal ideas with value and the fact of the concomitant behavior.[10]

In the writer's view, in dealing with this basic problem and in an effort, also, to achieve a synthesis of jurisprudential thought, *positive law is social conduct expressing norms that imply values, deviation from which, implying a judicial process, causes harms that are and must be met by the imposition of sanctions.*[11] In this perspective, law is not to be identified with the ideas it includes and expresses any more than the concept of a man or of a book is the man or the book.[12] That such conduct is, instead, an integration of the above elements is supported by the psychological theory that thinking, feeling, and willing are not separate faculties but that they coalesce in normal personality. Thus, a man performing an agreement has certain legal ideas in mind when he actualizes the value of keeping a promise and, at the same time, the movements of his body and some of the artifacts he employs are observable. The above theory is supported not merely on psychological grounds but by reference to the above-noted progress in social and ethical theory since Savigny and, especially, in this century.

In order to avoid serious misunderstanding, it is essential to keep in mind that the theory that positive law is a distinctive type of social conduct does not imply that the definition of "law" in terms of concepts or rules is incorrect in the practical realms discussed above. It is not a question of substituting the above definition of law for the established practical concepts. The new definition is part of the discourse of a theoretical discipline, and its compatibility with the practical definitions is reflected in that of the theoretical and practical motifs of the principal legal philosophies. In other words, what is involved is not merely the addition of a new definition of positive law to the existing practical ones. Instead, the "basic position" is that there are various aspects of the social reality of positive law which are emphasized for different purposes.

When positive law in the practical realm is not distinguished from law as social reality, irrelevant questions are raised. For example, Gray "refuted" Savigny's theory by citing conflicting States' laws concerning the acceptance of an offer.[13] But, at most, this indicates that law-as-conduct does not completely reflect or correspond with all of the State's positive laws; and, indeed, their interrelations are much more complicated than that. Certain important sectors of social action reflect wide agreement on basic values from which many of the State's rules can be derived, and still others are found as logical implications or extensions from them. There are also lacunae filled by creative legislators and judges influenced in varying degrees by social conduct. There are technical rules and so on. This problem will be discussed later.

The first place to look for evidence of the social reality of law is in one's personal experience. If one has witnessed or been the victim of a crime of violence, he probably discovered that the bare ideas, the relevant rules, of law fused with feeling and tendencies to act. In any case, everyone has sometime encountered what Durkheim called *représentations collectives*, including popular attitudes expressing legal ideas—"normative facts" which influenced his conduct much more than did physical objects in the environment. These cultural phenomena are a product of human interactions, and they condition succeeding generations to whom the traditions are transmitted. What, in legal practice, are rules or concepts of law are, thus, in actual experience clothed with the fact of feeling and tendencies to act.[14]

If, guided by the insight derived from personal experience, we study preliterate societies and observe what happens when various harms are committed, our attention is also drawn to certain recurrent conduct. It may be urged that the law is in the minds or memories of the people. But that is suggested by the practical, traditional meanings of law; and the question for consideration is, what is the soundest inference to be drawn from a sociological viewpoint? From that perspective, the plain fact is that what we have presented is certain social action—"conforming" conduct, the deviation and the conduct expressed in the group's reaction, which includes both judging and imposing sanctions.

The next objection may be that a rule must exist before any conduct can be illegal or antisocial and that this establishes the priority and autonomy of the concept of law. This raises a difficult problem and, facing it, one might first ask whence and how did this concept or standard come to be constructed and, more particularly, could it have been conceived if there were not realities from which the standard could be derived? [15] If this be granted, the issue becomes whether these "realities" are only social norms or whether, in a sociological perspective, they comprise the conduct which expresses those norms.

It is, moreover, far from self-evident that thought must always precede conduct.[16] Conduct may sometimes be a spontaneous affair in which consciousness is instantaneously fused with movement. But even if thought always preceded conduct, this would not determine the sociological view of positive law. Regardless of the origins of law, in any sense, in the social disciplines social action is the prime datum, the minimal unit. And despite the fact that philosophers begin and often end with thinking, action is the more defensible starting point in law and social science; it is also the necessary point of validation of the relevant knowledge. The legal norms can be "abstracted" from the fused social reality of law to form the concepts by reference to which conformity and deviation are judged.[17] Thus, juridical science, pursuing the practical purpose of determining when and upon whom sanctions are to be imposed, defines positive law in terms of delict and sanction. But these practical legal concepts attain fuller significance when seen in relation to the relevant social reality.

Legal institutions have their roots in the experience of individuals socialized in a process of personal interactions. Long before the legislature, the judiciary, and the corps of enforcement officers became specialized in anything like their current forms, customary law prevailed as the dominant, perhaps exclusive, type of law. In its social reality, it comprised the distinctive conduct previously described, and (not inconsistently with recent anthropological rejection of the "hard cake of custom") conformity prevailed. This was the necessary prerequisite to the abstraction of rules from the conduct, forming the conceptual standards employed by officials concerned with deviation. Viewing the concept apart from the conduct which expressed the norm, holding the concept in mind to judge deviation, is necessary in practice. But that abstraction and that practice do not alter the reality.

The dominance of the tradition that positive law is a rule or concept, hardly challenged from Plato to the rise of modern social science and still widely accepted, exerts strong pressure to limit "law" to norms, rules, or concepts. This disposition to conform to the practical meanings of "law" has been expressed in such terms as "law-*in*-action" and the like. It has advanced to the point of distinguishing the legal concept, as a mental construct, from the norm expressed in social action. This is the present position in sociology and social psychology, which adhere to Weber's theory of "conduct oriented to norms," [18] where it is the norm, not the conduct, that is taken to be law. Although this represents an important advance over the prior conceptualism of juridical science, it is still indefensibly tied to that view of "law," since the relevant perspective is sociological, not practical. For these reasons, the social reality of law is not solely the norms internalized in the conduct; it is the whole of the conduct which includes and expresses those norms and, also, has the other characteristics stated above.

In analyzing that reality, the norm can, of course, be distinguished from the other components of the conduct. But this does not describe the norm. To describe it one must take account of its coalescence with the factual side of conduct and the concomitant actualization of value.[19] Thus, too, one could emphasize the behavioral side of the conduct described above, but an accurate description of the behavior would need to relate it to the legal ideas and values expressed. We deal with a unit, and the only way to describe any essential phase accurately is to take account of its integration with the other essential components with which it is fused. For the social reality of law is different from, it is "more than," the sum of its parts; the abstraction of the parts should not be confused with the description of them.[20] In sum, what is discovered in social phenomena, that is, "what they are," depends, in part, on what is sought, and that is determined by the theory which guides the search. If the guiding perspective of a theory of law is sociological, one finds certain social conduct, the integration of the components described above.

The above theory of positive law may contribute to the solution of one of the most difficult problems of jurisprudence, the much-discussed dualism of the Is and Ought of law. For while an Is conclusion cannot be logically derived from Ought premises nor an Ought conclusion from Is premises, a solution is indicated in the above theory because the value and the factuality of law coalesce in the specified on-going conduct as it moves towards its goal. This parallels natural law philosophy which posits fact and value in the cosmos—both are "given" from the outset. However cogent this may be in an abstract context, it finds more persuasive or, at least, more direct expression in a jurisprudence where distinctive human conduct rather than the cosmos or nature is taken as the ontological realm of positive law. One can understand the value of certain human action even if he has difficulty in grasping the metaphysics of a realm of independently subsisting values. In either case, one avoids the fallacy of reducing the normativity of law to fact as well as the above logical difficulty of conceptualist jurisprudence in dealing with the Is and Ought of law.

Accordingly, the above theory of law also rejects the behaviorism which treats human conduct as wholly factual. Human conduct does not exist solely in the sense or ways that inanimate things and lesser animals exist; description of it in those senses is always incomplete and it may also be inaccurate. For human conduct manifests a significant degree of free decision, implying its rationality. That is one reason why the above definition of positive law specifies that sanctions are and *must be* imposed—a statement that is necessary and compatible with the freedom of human conduct. At every split second, any action, including that of persons in "society" as well as that of the judges of deviation and the corps of ministerial officers, is poised and appreciably undetermined. It can proceed towards a chosen objective, it can stop short of that, or it can alter its course in various ways. This conduct has been described in terms of "tension between values and facts," between the pull of the Ought and the inertia of fact.[21] However difficult it is fully to describe this process of actualizing values, the static, mutually exclusive implications of conceptualist Is-Ought postulation are thus transcended. A realistic view of such conduct, informed by introspection and observation, finds it normative as well as factual.

The State's Law and Law-as-Conduct

It is often assumed that social conduct more or less "conforms" to legislation and judicial decisions. But what is known about this[22] or about the effect of social action on the judges? And what of the sanctions-process and its interrelations with the judicial process and social action?

Ehrlich perceived that "legal propositions" were derived from living law,[23] continuing in this respect the theory of the German historical school. But for him, as well as for Weber, juridical science and the sociology of law existed in separate compartments —the former seeking "correct" solutions, while the latter was interested in social action "oriented" to legal norms. In the preceding discussion, that part of juridical science concerned with common concepts ("comparative law" in the conceptualist sense) was brought within the scope of a humanistic legal sociology, marking a sharp departure from the above theories of legal sociology. But in the lack of knowledge of the interrelations of the State's laws and law-as-conduct, the legal scholar can only hope that the work he devotes to the discovery and elucidation of common concepts is somehow relevant to what actually happens.[24]

In certain areas, of course, social conduct and the judicial process are plainly in close correlation and they may also be in common deviance from the statutory law. For example, public attitudes regarding divorce have resulted in frequent falsification in order to meet the statutory requirements, and the courts acquiesce in this practice. There is also common knowledge of the wide gap between the former laws prohibiting the manufacture and sale of alcoholic liquor in the United States and social conduct; but here, many, perhaps most, courts supported the statutory law. It is well known that many sexual offenses are very frequently committed and that only a minute fraction of them are prosecuted; and the situation is similar as regards known embezzlers. In some countries the government is controlled by a small elite claiming a superior cultural status, and both legislation and judicial decision are sometimes imposed upon a reluctant community.

On the other hand, it seems probable that judicial decision, the "custom of the courts," frequently influences public attitudes, business transactions, and other social conduct. Following legislation and decisions, lawyers report required changes to corporate and other clients and they organize enterprises to accord with the State's laws. Even in areas where public opinion is bitterly opposed to decisions that require new patterns of conduct, the prestige of the courts exerts some influence. Where basic values are involved, as in major crimes against the person, close correlations among these variables may be expected, but it should not be forgotten that "society" is an abstraction and that large associations, for example, labor unions and business corporations, may be influenced by decisions that seem remote from the interests of the "general public."

Current social theory is not very critical of such notions as "oriented to law" and "internalized," and it indiscriminately intermingles traditional thinking about "law" with social research. Thus, deviation is regarded as contradictory to and outside "law" which must, on that premise, be defined solely in terms of conformity. But in terms of the theory of law as social reality, presented above, deviation must be brought within a descriptive definition of "positive law." Starting with the practical juridical definition of "law" in terms of delict and the imposition of the sanction, this theory articulates the references of these concepts in terms of social conduct—deviation and the conduct of enforcement officers imposing privations. Since the perspective is sociological, not practical, positive law cannot be confined to those limits. Delict implies conformity and from a sociological viewpoint which centers on social action, so-called "conformity" is at least as important as deviation. In other words, since the sanction is an essential component of law, "law" cannot be defined without reference to the delict, or violation of law. A violation of law is obviously not conformity to law, but the sociological definition of law, for the reasons stated above, must take account of both.

For the various reasons discussed above and further elucidated in the following chapters, it is necessary to distinguish the laws of the State from the social reality of law and to conclude, also, that within the field of legal sociology and the wider one of social theory it makes a great deal of difference whether law is taken to mean norms which are "internalized" or to which conduct is "oriented" or whether law consists of social conduct expressing norms that imply values, deviation from which (implying a judicial process) causes harms which are and must be met by the imposition of sanctions (implying a regular pattern of imposing disvalues).

With reference to the interrelations of the State's laws and law as social reality, perhaps enough has been said to indicate that it is possible and necessary to go much further than recognition of truisms about a minimal consensus regarding basic values; socio-legal research should therefore construct bridges between judicial decisions, legislation, the sanctions-process, and social action. In planning such studies, one might plot a set of possible interrelations, using the State's law and law-as-conduct as the principal variables which exhibit degrees of "coincidence" (complete, wholly separate, slight, or substantial) in particular areas at specified times and places. Such studies would also involve the relation of positive law, in the above sociological sense, to its social context.

Social Context

There is nothing in physical nature, in sheer fact, which makes some things primary or focal and other things contextual. When human beings are sufficiently interested in something, that becomes "the center," and anything else can qualify only as its context. Thus when law, however its character and province are determined, is placed in a social context, it is related to data that are not law. But the fact that a human interest is important in the determination of this question does not imply that it is the only factor involved or that all decisions in this regard are equally sound. The test is increase in knowledge.

The practical perspective of lawyers is focused on the words comprising rules of law; hence, the usual connotation of "context" is the verbal one implied in the reference of words to their grammatical order and their relation to other words, including sentences and paragraphs. Enlarging the verbal context, lawyers take account of more remote sentences in a statute, instrument, or recognized antecedent statements, for example, in a legislative hearing, until, given the instant problem and purpose, they are satisfied with the meaning of the words in issue. A wider context of ordinary speech and professional usage is implied; and, of course, legal terms, unlike those of mathematics, refer to certain facts, actions, and the qualities of things, hence, the elucidation of legal terms always involves some knowledge of those referents. As was seen above, juridical science, usually explicated in "legal positivism," raises this professional work to a jurisprudential level in abstract terms which are universally applicable.

When legal comparatists speak of placing legal rules in social contexts, the initially suggested image is, therefore, that of placing legal terms or ideas in social contexts. Little has been written by them to indicate just what this means or involves, or how it is to be employed to increase knowledge of law.

The first step in that direction is recognition that not only are there verbal contexts, there are also factual contexts. For example, a chimney is located in relation to a fireplace and house; an airport is related to planes and cities, and so on. We may not often speak of placing a man in a social context—that is the vocation of novelists. But we frequently do that, consciously, if a special interest is aroused, or unconsciously, as we come to know a person. The personality of the man in his library, which contains as many philosophical as legal works, acquires still another dimension when he is found in the circle of his family; if, calling upon him one day, we surprise him at the piano playing Bartok, we realize that the meaning of men and things located in expanding factual contexts has vast potentialities.

In everyday life, things are placed in many different contexts without restriction by legal practice; and the arts, humanities, and sciences contribute to our knowledge of them. From the recognition of the most primitive qualia of experience to the farthest reaches of science and philosophy, the mind makes comparisons that place things in various contexts. The native quest for intelligibility culminates in the indicated types of knowledge which include and depend upon the construction of congruent contexts.

Although law is conceptual in the practical connotation of "law and social context," the reference of legal comparatists to problem-solving, the function of laws, and to law as a social institution implies a sociological perspective. If one follows the implications of these references, as was seen above, "comparative law," fully articulated, is humanistic legal sociology which includes the elucidation of common concepts. Answers to the question, what is the context of laws, thus depend upon whether one is engaged in a theoretical inquiry or in the solution of practical problems, upon what questions should have been asked, given the perspective, and, finally, upon the relevant realities. I have discussed the reasons why, in comparative legal study viewed as a social discipline, positive law is certain conduct, a social reality.

The widest congruent definition of the social context of positive law, thus defined, would include not merely the immediate surroundings evident to common experience, but everything that law-as-conduct has produced and everything that has influenced or determined that conduct. Among the latter are physical and biological forces involved in human "definitions of social situations." There are purely social forces of an almost equally inexorable character for societies that survive, for example, institutions assuring the protection of women and the survival of children, the division of labor, some distribution of property, the transmission of tradition, and limitation on the use of force and fraud in interpersonal relations. Accordingly, "social context" also means social reality, especially social action, articulated in various processes and institutions, including the nonhuman environment so far as it is involved in these social data. In distinguishing the social context from the social reality of law, it is necessary to take account of the positive law of subgroups, on the one hand, and of the areas of privilege (liberty) and power on the other hand. The construction of social contexts would vary in relation to the problems investigated; and there are other considerations which will be noted later.

The mystery of placing legal terms or concepts in vague social contexts is thus replaced by insight into the interrelations of definite social realities. The "function of law" becomes meaningful as the function of certain human conduct, and the value of law and the connotations of "problem-solving" likewise acquire realistic meanings. We look for the origins of similar types of law-as-conduct, we reconstruct similar socio-legal events in detailed case-histories, and in the other previously indicated ways we seek knowledge of similar aggregates of law-as-conduct in various societies; law, thus viewed, is placed in equally "substantial" social contexts.

If we consider the above discussion with reference to the basic problem of the "comparability of data," we see implied there the requirement that there must first be a definite perspective (selected from the principal perspectives which have influenced definitions and theories of positive law) which, in general terms, indicates the criteria of cogent comparison. The next, more particular finding, compatible with the relevant given perspective, was that the inclusive results of the described comparative study comprise a humanistic legal sociology; and this again implies a congruent subject matter. This subject matter was found to be distinctive social conduct—a coalescence of legal ideas, values, and facts; these indicate the criteria of comparison more definitely. The remaining problem concerns the analysis of these phases of the subject matter in terms that are helpful in research. Certain sociological theories to which we now turn are especially suggestive in this regard.

SOCIAL STRUCTURE, FUNCTION, AND PROBLEM-SOLVING

Social Structure

Modern social science borrowed three fundamental ideas from nineteenth-century biology: structure (morphology), function (physiology), and development (genetics). The aptness of these notions in biology seems obvious, for example, the heart and lungs have definite form, and they function to preserve life—the maintenance of the structure of the organism. It is little wonder, in view of the progress of biology and the suggestiveness of these concepts, that social scientists have sought to apply them to their disciplines.

That literal efforts to do so are misdirected is shown in the distinctiveness of social action, especially in discovery and problem-solving which actualize valuable goals. The heart and lungs do not take "leaves of absence," but a Thoreau may choose a hermit's life. Human sociability also differs markedly from the gregariousness of bees and ants.[1] And the most typical human traits, as the discussion of problems and the protection of the rights of minorities, which are essential in democratic societies, are wholly irrelevant to organic processes.

These differences, however, do not imply that analogies drawn from biology may not be profitably employed in the social sciences. For example, if one visits a family, a court, and a labor union, he recognizes immediately that they are different groups and he also learns from repeated observations that there is an "identity" which characterizes each group and persists even though its membership and location are altered. These distinctive traits of social groups and social actions comprise their structure. There is wide agreement in sociology, anthropology, and comparative politics that the components of social structure are norm, status, and role.[2] A status is a position held by an actor, role specifies the action required of anyone holding that position, and "status-role" combines the static and the dynamic connotations of those terms.[3] Norms render social actions intelligible and supply the basis for expectations regarding the conduct of persons in a known culture. Professor Sorokin's statement that *"law-norms are the essence—the skeleton, the heart, and the soul—of any organized group or institution"* [4] may seem exaggerated unless one bears in mind that "law-norms" are not restricted to the State's law. In any case, it can hardly be doubted that they are among the most important structural features of social actions, groups, and institutions.[5] In the larger view of this lawyer-sociologist, the "structure of sociocultural interaction" includes (1) human beings who interact, (2) norms, values, and other meanings, and (3) social actions and material things (artifacts). The first of these, connoting "personality," is the particular subject of psychology; the second, comprising culture, is central in anthropology; and the third constitutes society, the field of sociology.[6] In fact, all three are interrelated in any cogent analysis of social action.

Certain parallels and differences between the theory of positive law discussed above and these sociological theories are apparent. "Conduct," in the above theory of law, obviously implies persons or "actors" and, articulated in thousands of social actions, it also includes many status-roles, official and lay. To the legal norms may be added nonlegal norms and other meanings, especially in the analysis of social contexts, without incompatibility with the above theory of law. On the other hand, this theory differs from current sociological theories with reference to the meaning and place of "values" in social action, and correspondingly, as regards "function" and other important concepts. These questions will be discussed later.

Law-as-conduct, of course, includes the official structures of the judicial process and the sanctions-process.[7] These are interrelated in various ways, for example, the latter is subordinate to the former in the hierarchy of authority, being "ministerial" to its actualization, while the efficacy of the decisions depends upon that of the law-enforcement. So, too, the official aggregates are in various ways interrelated with social "conformity" and deviation. The analysis of law-as-conduct and social context thus requires the specification of social actions, transactions, groups, and institutions [8] distinguished in terms of certain norms and other meanings, status-roles, and values.

Sociological analysis of the norms deals with two questions and terminates, first, in locating many of the State's laws in a wider field that includes the substantively similar norms of various subgroups. If "sovereignty" is treated either as formal or as a degree of power and the State's sanctions include measures other than physical force,[9] the laws of the State are not substantively different from those of various subgroups. The principal issue in this regard concerns the alleged "inexorable imposition" of the State's sanctions, which is sometimes expressed as the State's monopoly of "legitimate force." But it is doubtful that the sanctions-processes of all other associations (for example, the Mafia, the family, and various other legal groups) are substantively different.[10] It may be tenable and even helpful in social research to employ a set of criteria to distinguish the State's laws substantively from those of various subgroups.[11] Such criteria might be the rank of the laws in the hierarchy of authority, the inclusiveness of the State's interests, the relatively organized arrangement of its laws, the formality of its procedure, the idea or claim of inexorability, as contrasted with the theoretical privilege of withdrawing from other associations, and the lack or lesser degree of the other characteristics, noted above. But this would be misleading unless the above-indicated facts concerning the problematical issues were also described.

Sociological analysis of norms also distinguishes positive laws, in the above enlarged sense which includes the laws of subgroups, from mores, folkways, and fashions; [12] and it concentrates on the sanction.[13] Sanctions are usually viewed from the perspective of society and in terms of the social purposes they are intended to serve. But they have different meanings for various offenders, injured persons, the sanctions-corps, and private protective agencies. They also act as a limitation on the proscription of harms. The subtlety of some harms, the greater efficacy of other controls, and the vagaries of public opinion, for instance, regarding false commercial advertising, condition the proscription of harms because effective sanctions are not available or are not desired. In any case, the sanctions-process is viewed sociologically as including especially the conduct of the ministerial corps of officials and their counterparts in subgroups in interaction with other "variables." [14] What we visualize, in sum, is a large network of aggregates of law-as-conduct, official and lay, interrelated among themselves and, also, with numerous nonlegal aggregates—the "social context."

Current sociological theories usually ignore the valuational aspect of social action or they "reduce" values to psychological attitudes or other facts. [15] But values are principles of social order upon which norms and status-roles depend for their meaning. For example, unless the values implied in deviation are considered, the variety and refinement of the sanctions of modern legal systems are hardly intelligible. The importance of values in determining the meaning of norms has long been recognized in legal practice, for example, as regards the construction of legal instruments and statutes. It is illustrated in every socio-legal action, as in the restraint exercised by police and prosecutors. Isolated, the norms imposing limitations on persons seeking to protect the community would be irrational, but related to certain democratic values, their meaning is immediately understood. [16] Values, of course, also suggest motives as well as the basis of the explanation of social actions opposed to individual desires, habits, and preferences.

To know that aggregates of distinctive socio-legal conduct are the ultimate units of the subject matter is extremely important in the construction of a congruent discipline; but more than this is sought by social scientists. They wish to explain these phenomena precisely and to organize the relevant knowledge. This requires firm, significant classification, and that, in turn, depends on stable phenomena. Despite the fact that nature is continuous, it is relatively easy to ignore the subtleties of intermediate links and to construct firm classifications of stable units. [17] This not only allows significant comparisons to be made, it also provides the basis for scientific generalization; in chemistry it is the foundation upon which that body of scientific knowledge has been erected. But if classification is impossible, scientific generalization is impossible, and to hold that only a very vague classification is discoverable implies the limitations of additional general knowledge. This raises a very difficult problem in comparative sociolegal study, indeed, in all social science. One important step towards its solution is the theory of social structure discussed above. "Social typology" carries this effort forward to more precise classification, as the basis of comparison. Before discussing the relevant sociological theories, it may be helpful to note some parallel efforts by legal comparatists.

Legal Systems

As working comparatists, legal scholars usually seek "common concepts" among parts of a branch of the law of countries reflecting a relatively homogeneous culture. When larger problems involving the law of many countries are considered, legal comparatists, reflecting historical traditions, are apt to think in terms of certain "legal systems."

Arminjon, Nolde, and Wolff, however, criticize classifications of legal systems based on geography, race, codified law, case-law, and so on, because they are internally inconsistent.[18] They limit their program to the private law of modern civilizations and, emulating the highly successful classification of languages by philologists, they select the genealogy of various bodies of modern private law as the basis of their legal classification. By reference to this criterion, they find that there are seven families of private law—the French, German, Scandinavian, English, Russian, Islamic, and Hindu; and within each of these are various derivative systems. They discuss the diffusion of these bodies of law, especially those of European origin, and emphasize the fact that peoples who are far apart and very different as regards their ideas, manners, beliefs, and economy are governed by identical or very similar laws. This implies that cultural criteria are irrelevant, which accords with the learned authors' view of comparative law as a "dogmatic" practical science. Indeed, they emphasize the fact that a relatively backward society may have laws which are more advanced than those of France or England because the former adopted recent improvements, e.g., in procedure. This is said to support the position that comparative study should be focused on law, not on the degree of civilization of a society.[19]

The above fact may be relevant to wide generalizations about "legal systems"; but it is submitted that the above classification is unsuited to the needs of comparative study because it rests solely on the origin of the various bodies of private law. Things may have a common origin and differ in the most important respects, as do men and anthropoid apes; conversely, very similar institutions or cultural traits may have very different origins. In linguistics and biology, a single origin is employed to explain common characteristics among the data, but in the absence of any specification of similarities among the laws designated "French" and so on, knowledge of their origin cannot serve this purpose.

In rejecting classifications of "legal systems," however, the above authors made an important advance. "Legal system" implies that certain laws are logically organized, and in the philosophy of science, "system" connotes a well-knit, deductively manipulable organization of compendent propositions. Distinctive rules and concepts derived from Roman law are reflected in the laws of European countries, and there are certain codes which are to some extent "organized" or "systematic." But while these terms may be useful as general references, to indicate various degrees of organization, the assumption that the whole of any nation's laws, or even of a branch of that law, can in its totality be made the basis of comparative study clouds the problem of comparability. It mistakes what is at best a loose characterization and a traditional usage for a sound foundation of research. A classification of "legal systems" implies not only that all the national "bodies" of law included within each "system" are significantly similar but also that each of them differs importantly from the "bodies" of law in the other "systems." But none of these assumptions has been established, nor are they very plausible.

The above authors also state, as other writers have pointed out, that Islamic law had its source in the Koran and is based on theology. But Islam shares the Old Testament with the West, and Hindu and so-called "Western" law have also been influenced by religion. The abandonment of religion as a basis of classifying "legal systems" does not, of course, exclude the use of religion or particular religions in a classification of types of law, some of which might include parts of Islamic, Hindu, and Western law within the same class. A significant instance of the use of religion in comparative sociological analysis is Max Weber's study of the growth of modern capitalism, in which he compared Eastern societies with Western societies before and after the rise of Calvinism among the latter.

The above learned authors characterized Hindu law as structurally and technically primitive. This also suggests an apt basis of classification. For degree of systematization is a cultural trait which, unlike "legal system," is sufficiently definite and meaningful, for example, as an index of the state of scientific thought, to supply a criterion for comparative study. It accords with the premise of "comparative law," viewed as humanistic legal sociology, that the criteria of classification and the bases of comparability are cultural ones.[20]

For this reason, the approach of Professor René David to the above problem offers greater promise. In his *Traité* (1950), published in the same year as the above treatise, he classified legal systems by reference to their underlying "ideologies," distinguishing Western law, based on Christian morality, democratic liberalism, and a capitalistic economy, from Soviet and socialist law, based on a pervasive state economy and, presumably, also lacking the other noted criteria. He, too, distinguished Islamic law by reference to the religion of Islam, added Hindu law, which reflects a still different philosophy and, finally, he characterized Chinese law as "secular."[21] Accordingly, M. David rejected the frequent opposition of Continental law and common law, pointing out that they do not differ ideologically, but only as regards matters of technique.

In a recent essay, however, M. David abandoned the position he maintained in the *Traité*, on the ground that non-Western countries are also democratic, the economy of Western nations is becoming increasingly socialistic, and Christian morality has spread to many Afro-Asian countries. He now holds that the soundest basis for classifying legal systems is adherence to the "rule of law," and that this sets Western law apart from other law.[22]

That adherence to "the rule of law" is a very apt and important cultural criterion upon which to base comparative study seems evident. There are, to be sure, certain problems which render its application far from simple. For example, conflicting interpretations are given the "rule of law" by scholars in different cultures; some dictatorial regimes, such as Fascist Italy, adhered to "the rule of law" in a positivistic sense, while Denmark departed from it in certain respects, and so on.[23] And, because no research which would satisfy the standards of the best current social science has been undertaken regarding adherence to "the rule of law," we still lack definite knowledge of the similarities and differences in even French, English, and American law in this respect.[24]

A significant approach to this problem was recently suggested by Justice Vivian Bose, who classified countries into six groups on the basis of their adherence to "the rule of law."[25] First, he said, are the Communist regimes "which do not believe in it at all in the sense in which we do"; and distinguished, as a potential adherent to it, was Yugoslavia. At the opposite extreme, he placed countries (most of the countries of Western Europe, the United States, Canada, and New Zealand) where the rule of law "is so firmly established that it is quite unthinkable that it will ever be changed in any of its fundamentals." Between these extremes, there is, he said, "an almost infinite variety that is not easy to classify." India, Malay, Jordan, and some African countries, especially Nigeria, have absorbed "the rule of law" to a considerable degree. Falling short of that are Burma, Pakistan, and Turkey, although they show promise in this regard since large, influential groups support the rule of law there. Finally, in Indonesia and Guinea, there are dictatorships and only a facade of law, while in the Congo there is "complete chaos."

Although many questions could, no doubt, be raised regarding this classification, it represents a sound approach to the ordering of diverse data, which will be discussed later. It also suggests a method of solving the problem which impelled M. David to abandon the criteria he had employed in his *Traité*. His insight that morality, economy, and democratic constitutional government [26] are influential cultural factors, significant in comparative legal study, can hardly be doubted. And the fact that Western and non-Western countries share the same values and that private economic enterprise and liberal democracy are found in many widely separated parts of the world is not a valid ground for abandoning these important criteria as bases for such study.

What needs to be abandoned, it is submitted, is the inherited assumption that "Western," "non-Western," "European," and "legal system" are apt criteria for classifying socio-legal data for the purposes of comparative study. It is not suggested that the legal culture of some Western countries does not differ very significantly from that of many other countries,[27] for example, as regards relatively organized "bodies" of law, close adherence to "the rule of law" interpreted in terms of the value of personality, functioning bills of rights, and so on. What is implied is that these and other significant criteria must be employed critically and that the above omnibus notions should therefore be abandoned or used merely as convenient linguistic devices in preliminary references, not as bases of comparative research.

This is the direction urged by historians and social scientists intent on transcending cultural parochialism.[28] They recognize that if "Western" is taken to mean European, Christian and industrialized, and "non-Western" the lack of these, many obstacles are raised to classification in those terms. For example, "European" has many meanings, and there do not seem to be any "essentially European" traits. The same difficulty concerns "Western" and disputes whether Russia is a European country.[29] The Philippines and Korea, which are said to be Christian nations, and Japan, which is industrialized, raise other questions, while "non-Western" poses additional problems because of the great differences among cultures to which that label is popularly attached. In sum, "legal system," "European," "Western," and "non-Western" cannot support the classification of data for purposes of research. Legal scholars interested in the comparability of their data should look in other directions. That direction taken in contemporary sociological theories of "social structure," articulated in the more precise terms of "social typology," seems quite promising.

Social Typology

In the 1900 Paris Congress, Tarde suggested a classification of types of law as the basis of a comparative sociology.[30] In fact, the employment of "types" is an ancient practice. An "ideal type" was used by Plato in his delineation of the *Republic*, which he applied in the *Laws*,[31] by Aristotle in his classification of types of polity, and by numerous successors. Kant's categories of the mind suggested the social objectification of mental constructs to Dilthey, who initiated the construction of social typologies in current social science.[32] But it was nineteenth-century biology, based on the classification of numerous definite forms,[33] which stimulated many efforts to articulate social typologies.[34]

Social scientists distinguish three kinds of "social type." First is the "classificatory type" or "pattern," [35] employed, for example, in biology and chemistry as the basis of the knowledge comprising those sciences. Second is the "ideal type," which exaggerates an aspect of the actual data; "economic man," "capitalism," "feudalism," and "introvert" represent major tendencies.[36] This sociological "ideal type" should not be confused with Plato's. The former is wholly empirical in intent and might be more aptly designated the "salient-feature type." There is, third, the "extreme type" previously noted and illustrated above in terms of extremes of knowledge—that of individuality and that of universal generality. Such comparison, as noted, requires at least three items (A is more like X than B is), and consists in ranging items in a series of gradations.[37] To the above types employed in current sociological theory should be added the "ideal type" constructed by Plato.[38] For example, an ideal of democratic law, or of an accused person's rights and resources, or the code of human rights of the International Commission of Jurists, not wholly realized in any country, could be significantly employed in comparative study.

Among the most notable efforts to construct social typologies were those of Emile Durkheim and Max Weber. Durkheim found the elementary "social unit" in the horde and, just as the cell combines to form more complex organisms, so, he thought, hordes combined to form, first, simple "mechanical" societies and then, as necessity gave rise to the division of labor, complex, "organic" ones. On this basis, he constructed a "classification of social types, 'social morphology.' "[39] Unfortunately, the generality of his constructs as well as the doubtful basis upon which they rest leave his classification in a programmatic stage.[40]

The most sustained effort to construct social typologies has been the work of Max Weber.[41] Weber was especially sensitive to the flow and interpenetration of social data, and his "ideal type," discussed above, fixed attention on salient criteria selected for their theoretical significance.[42] Weber shifted from large "holistic" types such as "capitalism" and "rationalism" to narrower types centered on individuals, their knowledge, and interrelations.[43] That Weber's typology marked an important advance in social science is indicated in its wide use by historians, economists, and other social scientists.[44] But his "ideal types" have been severely criticized and social scientists are far from having solved this basic problem.[45]

The construction of typologies to meet the requirements of comparability is tied to the problem of communication, of how to make explicit and definite what is now implicit and vague. If we appraise the above sociologists' contributions as sustained efforts to render communication clear and precise, there can be nothing but appreciation of them. Weber's "ideal types," for example, are specifications of meanings intended to improve the precision of his text. With meticulous care, he articulated the presuppositions, concepts, and criteria which guided his comparative research and in terms of which he made his report.

If we view the problem in this way, we see that types are implicit in any comparison and that they must have been operative as "concepts" or "classes" from the very beginning of serious thinking on any subject. The "classificatory type" denotes the "one among the many," the "sameness" apprehended in two or more items. The "extreme type" is equally traditional for it concerns the familiar recognition of differences in degree. Such comparison is not limited to very different kinds of data: comparison of a branch of law of two democratic countries would gain in significance if a third democratic country were added. The resulting increase in the number of combinations of similarity and difference would add an important dimension to comparative study. The "salient-feature type" is almost equally pervasive. It denotes the main "thrust" of large configurations or movements, as seen in relation to a particular theory. As Holmes might have said, it strikes at the jugular vein. Finally, the "ideal type," in its Platonic sense, reflects the mind's leap from partial achievement to perfection; and this type, too, cannot be barred from uninhibited thinking about human action. Because of their direct significance for law and government, emphasis was placed above on political values. But since law-as-conduct is a socio-cultural datum, other values are, of course, also important.[46] In any case, it should not be forgotten that social typologies are tools, aiding analysis and clarity, but subordinate to the cultural significance of the data.

In light of the above discussion, the problem confronting comparatists is how the current typologies can be improved and adapted to the needs of socio-legal research.[47] Since the legal norm is of central importance in social structure, it provides the principal clue to the attainment of these objectives; this implies reliance upon legal norms as basic in the definition of socio-legal types. What is wanted, at least initially, are precise socio-legal typologies which include particular types of contract, negotiable instrument, certain aspects of marriage, succession, voting, use of a civil liberty, and so on. Later, research might be based on the wider constructs discussed above in terms of transnational legal theory.[48] Secondly, the value of socio-legal action should be included in the construction of these types. Third, comparative socio-legal study might well concentrate, first, on a very few countries representing common and civil law, whose polities are plainly democratic. After a series of intensive, co-ordinated studies of aspects of these undoubtedly similar legal cultures, guided largely by specific socio-legal types, it should be possible to determine which criteria had proved useful and, also, to discover other likely ones which had been omitted. A consensus might be sought among scholars in those countries regarding the conclusions reached in such research. For once there is general recognition of the comparative discipline as humanistic sociology of law, there could be definite resort to apt methods of validation, and the continuity of research could also be assured. It is, however, in comparison of quite different legal cultures that the most serious problems are met. It would be highly problematical to compare the English judiciary with that in Russia, where judges are expected to implement the party's program,[49] on the assumption that substantially similar "data" were being studied. Where there is a great diversity in socio-legal institutions, comparison in terms of classificatory types becomes verbal, trivial, or misleading. Although these types can be constructed in terms sufficiently general to include all societies, as in anthropological research on the functions of institutions essential to survival, that can hardly suffice in the study of widely different legal cultures of advanced societies, for there, interest centers on something more than survival. It is not implied that there are no universal values,[50] but that all values, for example, those of the best democratic societies, are not universal and, also, that there are differences in degree and in the abundance and refinement of values which are very important.

In studies of legal institutions of widely different cultures, the area of comparison via the "classificatory type" is limited, and relatively large reliance must be placed on "extreme type" comparison. In the study of contracts or adherence to the "rule of law," one extreme might be a socio-legal type defined by reference to data in democratic constitutional states, and the other extreme would be a type that reflects the selected criteria in a minimal degree; ranged between those extremes would be a series of gradations. While estimates from the viewpoint of the usual classificatory type of comparison discourage study or lead to opposed conclusions,[51] the use of extreme types would often support comparison in the sense of placement in a series.

Sweeping appraisals of "legal systems" cast doubt even upon this type of comparison. For example, it has been claimed that Soviet law is "a new type of law," "essentially different from all types of law known to history." [52] The former Marxist inspired view saw only the withering away of an oppressive class instrument, and the abandonment of that ideology by Stalinist scholars was accompanied by the claim that Soviet law is "paternal." If this refers to the treatment of the peasant as "a child or youth to be trained, guided, disciplined, protected," [53] comparable data might be found in the resources supplied indigent persons, juvenile courts, constitutional safeguards protecting illiterate foreigners accused of crime, and the like. If the wider thesis noted above is maintained either on the stated ground or on the ground that a wholly "planned" economy and culture affect not only the State's laws but also law as social reality, comparative study must take particular account of the consequent differences among legal institutions.

Even greater difficulties are raised in a recent monograph by M. René Dekkers, who believes Communist society is democratic in the "Western" sense of that word. M. Dekkers assumes that in Communist states large numbers of persons participate voluntarily in various governmental processes.[54] He does not discuss civil liberties or the "counterweights" to their actualization,[55] the absence of opposition political parties, or the manufacture of opinion by an elite in absolute control of education and all the media of communication. Apparently, also, frequent executions in Russia for speculation and crimes against property, the activities of secret police, and so on do not affect the "wholly educational" [56] character of Soviet penal law. For other scholars, these facts raise such troublesome questions that even extreme type comparison may be excluded by the requirements of a legal sociology regarding the minimal characteristics of its subject matter. In any case, the necessity to limit comparative study to carefully selected segments of "legal systems" seems evident.

Accordingly, inquiry directed towards the discovery of apt areas for comparative research among widely different "advanced" cultures might consider:

(1) Procedural law with reference to the logic and methods of pleading and proof. This does not imply that ideologies, dictation to officials, and other political pressures do not influence administration, but that logic is universal.

(2) Problems which are very similar in all societies and where differences in values are not very significant, for example, the mechanism of traffic control, public health, and safety measures.

(3) Technical rules which concern specialized activities of associations remote from public participation.

(4) Most importantly, segments of customary law which, because they do not touch the interests of the ruling elite, have continued in their traditional significance. There are survivals of barter and exchange and of segments of private contract law, parts of tort [57] and criminal law, especially crimes against the person, and aspects of marriage and family law which have a long history and preserve their traditional meaning in many societies.

It is not implied that the above problems can be wholly isolated from the salient features of a culture [58] or that these basic factors do not to some extent affect whatever socio-legal aggregates are chosen for comparative study. It is therefore essential to supply a background of historical, social, and ideological detail as well as a description of important differences among the data. In so far as a generalization may be ventured, it is that analysis should be largely in terms of the whole configuration of the culture rather than in terms of "classificatory type" comparison. The "classificatory type" comparison, to a limited extent, may be apt, but it should be supplemented by "extreme type" comparison. The delineation of the whole configuration of a culture, of course, includes comparisons at every step, but the emphasis is on detail and on the interconnections of particular institutions comprising a distinctive whole. No neat "formula" can facilitate such work, but an appreciation of the cultural criteria of comparability, familiarity with the various methods of research, and use of the above modes of comparison seem plainly indicated.

While serious difficulties are involved in the study of widely different legal cultures, such study also has important advantages. What may otherwise be assumed regarding the comparability of laws is immediately recognized as requiring careful articulation. New problems can be discovered in such study and new phases of known problems can be more fully apprehended. Such studies would also develop proficiency in the methods of research that are required for the progress of the relevant socio-legal discipline. Finally, for these reasons, the study of socio-legal aggregates in cultures that are very dissimilar in important respects would stimulate a more critical study of relatively homogeneous legal cultures.

Function

In the 1900 Paris Congress, Saleilles urged study of the functions of laws in their social context; and Lambert's criticism of the prevailing conceptualistic study of legal codes [59] anticipated Pound's view of "mechanical jurisprudence." In the United States in the nineteen-thirties, "functionalism" became a synonym of "American Legal Realism" except, perhaps, that it reflected greater philosophical sophistication in its ties with operationalism and logical positivism. For example, when Felix Cohen wrote about functionalism in 1935, he took as his text Wittgenstein's thesis that "most propositions and questions, that have been written about philosophical matters, are not false, but senseless." Functionalism was thus a reaction against the "supernatural concepts" of traditional jurisprudence.[60]

Sixteen years later, however, in a review of *The Open Society and its Enemies*, Cohen criticized Popper's attack on Plato, Hegel, and Marx, emphasizing their "seminal ideas, insights, and quirks of perspective to those who seek a faint ray of light on the muddy conflicts of our world . . . [W]hat was significant about these philosophers," he continued, "was the questions they formulated, questions which have given new dimensions to our thinking. It is to Plato, as Popper admits, that we largely owe 'that great spiritual revolution, the invention of critical discussion.' " [61] The present purpose is not to suggest that conceptualism triumphed over functionalism in postwar American legal thought but, instead, to call attention to the present view of "functionalism" in social science.[62]

The hope of nineteenth-century scholars of discovering stages of social evolution by use of "the comparative method" did not materialize; and when Malinowski engaged in anthropological research, he sought functions in the correlation of existing practices or institutions and social needs—that is, the perspective shifted from genetic to theoretical explanation.[63] "Function" acquired various meanings: description of facts as opposed to barren conceptualism, the efficiency of an instrument to achieve a given end, manifest and latent consequences of social action,[64] correlations between various institutions, "relation to the social structure to the existence and continuity of which it makes some contribution," and still others.[65]

After a period of enthusiastic, if indiscriminate, cultivation of "functionalism," the theory met increasingly severe criticism. The most widely accepted view, the "maintenance of structure," was found to be both vague and inapt.[66] The survival of the structure of a biological organism has definite meaning, but societies may cease to exist because of conquest, revolution, or migration, while the individuals composing them remain very much alive. Moreover, societies do not have rigidly fixed structures but alter their form as problems arise.[67] The tendency to find essential functions in every aspect of culture, as required responses to social needs, was also criticized.[68] Perhaps most serious is the fact that since social action is dynamic, a description of it in terms of factual functions adds nothing and it may mislead in suggesting a bifurcation of the fused components of such action.

Accordingly, what may have sounded the death knell of functionalism as a special theory in American sociology was struck in the 1959 Presidential Address to the American Sociological Society by Professor Kingsley Davis.[69] After noting how difficult it is "to say *what* functionalism is," because each "camp" uses the term in various senses, while critics of functionalism were engaging in the same kind of sociological analysis as were its advocates,[70] he called attention to the sort of questions functionalists raise: What features of social organization are common to all societies? Why are they so widespread? "How do they mesh together?" How are parts of social structure exhibited in roles and attitudes and conduct? Professor Davis then pointed out that such inquiries are "central to sociological analysis" [71] and he concluded that "structural-functional analysis *is* sociological analysis." [72]

One may grant the validity of this criticism of functionalism within the framework of the rigorously empirical presuppositions of current social science. But there are two important questions to be considered regarding this estimate in a social science admittedly concerned with norms, the first of which concerns the role of ideas in social action. As we have seen, sociologists emphasize the fact that norms are basic in social structure, but they have not sufficiently implemented that insight.[73] They discuss "expectation" regarding other persons' conduct, but that obviously depends upon meanings—especially those of the legal norms. This tendency—to avow the importance of norms and, at the same time, ignore, exclude, or fail to elucidate the role of normative ideas in social action—is occasionally manifested in comparative legal study, where criticism of conceptualism sometimes goes to the extent of opposing it to functionalism, implying that the functions of legal institutions can be understood and adequately described without reference to legal concepts. This ignores the distinctiveness of socio-legal action.

The other equally important problem concerning functionalism has to do with the relation of social action to social ends. This was the direction taken by Durkheim in 1895 in defining "function" in terms of "the correspondence between it [an institution] and the needs of the social organism." [74] Durkheim's interpretation of values in terms of relevant social attitudes borders on objective ethical criticism, but his successors have been more insistent on the exclusion of valuation from social science. For example, Professor Davis, in his discussion of functionalism, was especially critical of the "moralizing" connotations of that notion and of its proximity to "the purposive and moralistic reasoning of ordinary discourse." [75] This represents a widespread tendency among social scientists.

Only some salient aspects of this large question can be discussed here.[76] Obviously, the purpose of social scientists is to acquire knowledge, not to engage in criticism. But can social action be understood unless it is viewed, in part, as expressing valuations more or less actualized in problem-solving? It is apparent in jurisprudence, at least, that this question is largely rhetorical because the complete exclusion of valuation is impossible, as the painstaking effort of Duguit illustrates. Influenced by Durkheim and Bernard, Duguit developed a theory of the function of law in terms apparently freed from any value-connotation. But while he carefully barred his door against any intrusion by values, he left the windows open to *solidarité sociale*, even urging the functioning "units" of the social "organism" to do everything they could to increase it. Similar, if occasionally better concealed, valuations are implicit in any meaningful social analysis.

In a very important sense, which legal comparatists have often employed, to state the function of an institution is to refer it to the attainment of valuable goals, not simply to survival. This meaning of "function" is commonplace in daily conversation and its exclusion from social science bars realistic description. For, as was seen above, valuation accounts for, and gives meaning to, the norms; it also provides explanations of social action in terms of motives. Thus, it is meaningful to say that the function of criminal law is to maintain and clarify a community's values, that the functions of individualized treatment of criminals are rehabilitation and more precise justice, and so on. Legal comparatists sometimes criticize an institution on the ground that it does not serve effectively or sufficiently to attain a given value or that a different value should be sought.[77] They may wish to go further, as did Saleilles, and derive a set of principles to guide legislation everywhere. Legal and political theorists have discussed the basic functions of law in terms of order, security, justice, and so on.

Unfortunately, as Maitland noted, social scientists do not study the experience of courts, recorded during many centuries, which shows that the best way to understand action is to take account of it as end-seeking. Although the objective of social science is, of course, explanation and description, not criticism or adjudication, valuation is a necessary intermediate "operation" to understanding and realistic description. A purely factual report which ignores the most distinctive aspects of social action actualizing values, without compensating for the vast compilation of detailed facts by producing the general knowledge that is sought, is not apt to be very interesting. Instead, the postulate that values are only factual preferences or attitudes[78] only bars an understanding of problem-solving as a creative act or discovery.

Any uninhibited effort to understand end-seeking action inevitably touches one's own values and, therefore, valuation. Valuation is a definite kind of experience which includes thinking, weighing alternatives, envisaging various possible consequences, and sacrificing some goals to promote others; and this is involved whenever one really "participates" in another person's valuations. It may be the case that one cannot fully "participate" in very unfamiliar social actions and that some of them are almost incomprehensible. But to the extent that one does understand social actions, he does so in the light of his own reasoned convictions. Just as one evaluates various possibilities in his own problem-solving, so, too, once that realm of experience is entered, there is no escape from critical evaluation even though that is only instrumental to the social scientist's final goal—knowledge and description. This implies that a realistic study of socio-legal institutions proceeds on the premise that to some extent "objective" truths are attainable, that there are better and worse ways of dealing with social problems, and that, in at least a relative sense, some problems are solved. It also corrects the static implications of "structure," "equilibrium," and "social typology" and provides for spontaneity and the functions of problem-solving in actualizing values.

Problem-solving

If research is kept on a purely factual level, with evaluation rigorously excluded, problems are "solved" by whatever controls are employed, that is, "solution" is reduced to factual concomitants or consequences, and the plain implication that a better condition has been produced is simply abandoned. In a purely factual view, there would be no difference between dealing with unconventional intellectuals by banishing them to distant labor camps and dealing with them by allowing them free speech. Indeed, the factual effects of the former method would be quantitatively superior (which again reveals the impossibility of eliminating valuation from significant social science!).

"Common problem" can be even more misleading than "solution." For example, the crime rate for certain offenses may be relatively low in dictatorial states, but it would be hardly relevant to say that there was no problem of crime there or that democratic states had a much greater problem. In democratic societies, "social problem" implies freedom not only to discover that there is a problem but also to discuss it.[79] In this context, it makes sense to say that there are better and worse ways of solving problems and to speak of the "function" of laws in relation to the values they reflect and serve. These terms would assume very different meanings if they were applied to what is done by experts manipulating human beings in an authoritarian culture. "Social problem" is an abstraction from realities that include positive laws. Unemployment, for example, does not concern only the operation of economic forces. It also involves the legal institutions of property and contract. Protection against contagious diseases is not solely a question of immunization. It involves legal access to drugs and the licensed practice of medicine. Thus, social problems are socio-legal valuational problems, and the significant interrelations of these factors is the goal of cogent analysis.

In comparing the solutions reached in various countries, it is necessary to recognize that different bodies of opinion are influential and that the attitudes woven into the problems are not easily changed because they have developed in the course of many years. In large measure they account for the fact that different solutions of the same type of problem have been reached in similar cultures. For example, although the French administrative courts are everywhere very highly regarded, an American scholar, after a study of *droit administratif*, might well conclude that the French specialized courts are best for France, while our unified courts serve our interests best.[80] In Anglo-American history, constitutional methods of controlling the executive were institutionalized at a relatively early date, as was the independence of the judiciary, while in France and other Continental countries, these were much later achievements and, in the meantime, reform took the direction of control of administration by the administration itself. The status-role of the executive and popular attitudes towards judges are thus outgrowths of long historical movements. In the light of the variety of these experiences, it is not easy to determine the criteria of "best solution."

Historical and cultural influences also engender professional attitudes that complicate objective appraisal. For example, Continental scholars sometimes state that their criminal law serves the principle of legality more effectively than does American law. In their view, codes and statutes are paramount. The relative freedom of Continental judges from precedent is taken to minimize the influence of case law; and, perhaps imperceptibly, this is also attributed to the common law. An American lawyer, on the other hand, appraises the "rule of law" by reference to its precise articulation in numerous binding decisions rendered in terms of specific facts. He might look with suspicion on the generalities of codes, the lack of attention to the facts in the cases, and the uncertain influence on trial judges of even the decisions of the highest Continental courts. Actually, case law is very important there,[81] and the attention given the treatises should also be considered. Any optimism regarding the immediate prospects of a "comparative science" must be tempered by the realization of how far we are from having acquired definite knowledge of this basic problem of judicial method. Indeed, it is a sobering thought to find that even scholars who may claim expert knowledge of foreign law and legal methods sometimes hold fast, without warrant, to the perspective of their native culture.[82]

Despite the above difficulties regarding "common problem" and "solution," these notions are very important in any discipline which pursues the implications of the "function" of laws beyond casual references to their "social context." If "function" is taken to refer to the actualization of the values implied in the normative structure of social action, it serves an essential purpose in the acquisition of the desired knowledge. Circumspectly formulated, the discovery and description of a common socio-legal problem would set the focal point on which legal scholars and social scientists could concentrate their respective researches, elucidating norms, employing apt typologies, and discovering and explaining other similarities in the structures and functions of socio-legal conduct actualizing values. The knowledge thus acquired would augment and enlighten that which has been previously discussed —cultural legal history focused on current similarities in concepts and institutions, knowledge derived from comparison of similar leading case-histories guided by social theory, from research based on transnational legal theory, and limited correlations between similar legal and nonlegal aggregates as well as limited trends. The resulting body of knowledge would make present comparative disciplines branches of a well-established humanistic sociology of law.

6

TOWARDS LEGALLY ORIENTED
SOCIAL SCIENCE

In light of the conclusions reached above, it seems evident that the future progress of comparative studies depends largely on mutual understanding among certain specialists of their respective contributions. Specialization has its virtue as well as its necessity, but it also has serious limitations. For, while legal comparatists make valuable contributions in elucidating the normative structures of social action, they leave untouched large areas of relevant social inquiry to which social scientists make particular contributions. Much more than the mere juxtaposition or addition of the results of these specialized types of scholarship is required if we are guided by the available social theory; and a principal purpose of the above discussion has been to delineate the total enterprise of socio-legal inquiry so as to indicate the respective roles which legal scholars and social scientists have in it. This implies that the basic need is the reorientation of the specialized disciplines to a common subject matter; in terms of the above analysis, that subject matter is the social reality of positive law. Significant steps taken in that direction by legal comparatists in their discovery and elucidation of common concepts and in their references to social context, function, institution, and problem-solving have been discussed above. Some wider implications of the above discussion for social science must now be considered.

The interest of anthropologists in comparative primitive law and that of political scientists in modern law and government suggest that the anthropology of law, political science, and, of course, the sociology of law may actually constitute or be reconstructed to constitute a single social discipline.[1] Extending beyond that is the question whether all social science should not be legally oriented. It is impossible to engage here in the extensive inquiry that would be needed to support this hypothesis, but some matters relevant to both of the above theses may be briefly considered.

There is, first, the large consensus previously noted among social scientists that legal norms are of primary significance in social action; and there is, next, the sociology of Durkheim and Weber. Durkheim built his sociology directly upon law, which he regarded as the best evidence of underlying attitudes. While this implies that law in a positivist sense is not an "ultimate" social datum, the relevant question is whether a sociological theory of law would not subsume what Durkheim, still viewing law "legalistically," allocated to *représentations collectives*. The decisive point is that, for Durkheim, the coerciveness of social facts was the essential attribute which distinguished them from nonsocial data; and any social pressure satisfied Durkheim's conception of the legal sanction. This implies that Durkheim's sociology is a sociology of law. Weber's sociology concentrated on social action, and there are, of course, many motives influencing such action besides the legal norms. But Weber held that positive law cannot be restricted to the laws of the State.[2] His interest in mental states, in the teleology of action, and so on also raise doubts regarding the current assumption that the sociology of law is only a branch of "general sociology."

There immediately arise, of course, questions regarding the sociology of art, the sociology of religion, and so on. But the study of culture is usually allocated to anthropolgy; if the above sociologies are therefore restricted to the study of social action, the place of nonlegal norms and their relation to legal norms must be dealt with. Thus the sociology of law is not a mere application of "general sociology" but has a central position in it. For example, social actions expressing legal privileges and legal powers including those having significance for religion and art, are not nonlegal but, as was seen above, they take their meaning from their relation to relevant laws. A legally oriented social science would no doubt treat "law" in various senses and in relation to other types of normative action. It would also need to consider whether "nonlegal institution" is an abstraction from social actions and aggregates which include legal norms or require that legal norms be taken into account. Some of these problems have been discussed by various scholars in terms of the relations of law and economics. The following discussion of political science may perhaps serve as an outline of an analysis which can be applied to the other social disciplines.

In this connection and in order to achieve a single perspective from which to view current social science, attention should first be called to the fact that anyone familiar with the dominant aspects of twentieth-century American jurisprudence would immediately recognize its counterpart in the European comparative law movement from Maine and the 1900 Paris Congress to the present time.[3] There were, of course, certain differences, for example, emphasis on "the comparative method" applied to legislation and on evolution in the European movement, as contrasted with emphasis on the judicial process and physical science in the United States. But these were only minor notes in what can now be recognized as a single symphony. The direction of world affairs since 1940 and, not least, the presence in this country of many able European comparatists have transformed the earlier, culturally limited constructions of a legal science into larger efforts reflecting a more inclusive perspective. For the various reasons discussed above, the European and the American movements may be combined to constitute a humanistic legal sociology.

If a single perspective is thus achieved in twentieth-century legal thought, the next step—from legal thought to social science —can easily be taken. For it requires no more than mere reference to Weber and Durkheim, the leaders of twentieth-century sociology, to Maine, Bastian, McLennan and Bachofen, who laid the foundations of cultural and social anthropology, to Bryce and Dicey, Hauriou and Duguit, Lowell, Goodnow, McIlwain, Dickinson, and many other distinguished political scientists, to indicate the importance of the contributions of lawyers to social science.[4]

In many countries, including most of Latin America, the sociology of law continues to be a major discipline among legally trained sociologists. In the United States, it has fallen between the professional stool of the law schools and that of the departmentalized education of sociologists who, caught in the powerful current of scientific methodology, forego the legal studies of their illustrious predecessors. Legal anthropology is a marginal topic in the United States although, fortunately, there is a steady stream of British contributions stimulated by a major interest of Malinowski and Radcliffe-Brown.[5] Accordingly, while there are, no doubt, many anthropologists and sociologists who might be enlisted in the social study of law, the largest immediate potentiality in the United States, in this regard, is in political science.

The situation in political science is difficult to assess and, of course, it differs widely among the various nations.[6] In this country, at least, it seems to be a fact that when political scientists reacted against the formalism of nineteenth-century studies of laws and constitutions, many of them excluded law from the field of political data. While their jurisprudential colleagues, who also rejected arid *Begriffsjurisprudenz*, were tied to the practice of law and thus to the necessity of coping with legal ideas, no similar condition tempered the reaction of these political scientists, and they embraced empiricism *con amore*. But whatever satisfaction positivist sociology, physical science, and psychoanalysis provided in reactions against formalism, they could not facilitate the discovery of the distinctive subject matter of political science; indeed, they seem rather to have diverted attention from that basic problem.

It is very significant, therefore, that in a thoughtful survey of the discipline, Professor Charles Hyneman finds that interest in the "government of the state (or legal government)" gives American political science its common character. It is "that part of the affairs of the state which centers in government, and that kind or part of government which speaks through law" which is "the central point of attention for American political science."[7]

Despite the authority and potential importance of this estimate, the current situation in American political science is an anomalous one. While it is unanimously agreed that formal studies of law and government are outmoded, at the same time, especially as regards American government, the exorcised legal formalism seems to be assiduously cultivated. Indeed, studies of Supreme Court decisions and the Bill of Rights by political scientists are sometimes more "legalistic" than are those by legal scholars. On the other hand, many political scientists engage in empirical studies, and in this scientifically oriented branch of the discipline, law is ignored or barely noticed. There is also considerable interest in political theories (especially those of the classical writers) which emphasize the practical, ethical aspects of politics. But although the products of these various efforts are voluminous, they are far from comprising a "full understanding of legal governments." [8]

There are, no doubt, many factors that influence American political science, which, like "sociology of law," includes more than one type of knowledge. But its unique, problematical situation can be accounted for only by the lack of an adequate theory of its subject matter. And if that subject matter is "legal government," it is the lack of a theory of law or of law and government which is congruent with the intent of social science that is the crux of the problem.

In the lack of such a theory, not only is the current uncertainty regarding "political data" inevitable but, in addition, very important problems are not recognized. For example, even as regards the American national government, "very little of what goes on there has as yet been described." [9] There has been very little study of the effect of judicial decisions on public action, or of how public policy has been altered thereby, or how legislators have been influenced by the courts, or of the social context of the judicial process,[10] or of American attitudes toward the Constitution, state constitutions, or courts, and so on.[11] The gravity of these lapses can hardly be doubted in view of "the central point of attention," and persistent inquiries by political theorists regarding the subject matter of politics make it abundantly clear that this is the major difficulty. They also reveal that the problem of comparability is not restricted to any particular social discipline.

Current efforts of political theorists to discover or determine "the fundamental units of analysis" have been recently discussed by a distinguished political scientist in terms of action, systems, decision-making, power, groups, political communications, and functions.[12] Some of these concepts have been discussed above and others will be considered shortly. Especially noteworthy is the fact that the word "law" is not mentioned in this author's essay despite the "common interest in legal government."

The theory of the subject matter of politics recently discussed by Professor G. A. Almond comes much closer to meeting the indicated requirements. Professor Almond states that his "conception of the distinguishing properties of the political system proceeds from Weber's definition—the legitimate monopoly of physical coercion over a given territory and population." [13] In a more recent discussion of "adequate definitions of politics and the political," Professor Almond states that he recognizes the validity of the criticism that Weber's definition would exclude societies where there is no monopoly of the legitimate use of physical force, but he rejects a wider definition of "political" in terms of "coercive sanctions, of which force is the extreme form," because it does not specify what "coercive and other sanctions are" or take account of the sanctions-corps. He concludes by stating that he would enlarge Weber's definition "to include types of political organization other than the state" but he holds fast to "legitimate physical compulsion" on the ground that "only by such a specific definition" can we "distinguish political systems from other social systems." [14]

This theory of the subject matter of political science remains substantially as Weber formulated it since he did not restrict "law" to the laws of the State. [15] Its principal departure from Weber's theory, although conformity to it in this respect was assumed in the above political theory, concerns the restriction of legal sanctions to "legitimate force." But these and other questions which may be raised in the light of criticism of Weber's theory and subsequent advances in the sociology of law should not obscure the significant fact that the identity of political science and the sociology of law is clearly implied in this theory of the subject matter of politics. If the emphasis is shifted from "the State" to social action oriented to legal norms, including those of subgroups, which is where Weber placed it, we are led again to the quest for a theory of law which is compatible with both the perspective of a social science and the "common interest" of political scientists.

More particularly, the implications of the above chapters for political and other social science are:

1. All societies are legal organizations—*ubi societas, ibi ius.* While this implies that the State's laws must be studied, it is law as distinctive conduct articulated in the socio-legal aggregates discussed above, which is the core of political data; and by like token, political science is knowledge of that law and of other relevant social action.

2. Political science as well as the political theory which emphasizes the ethical, practical side of politics should be as precise as possible, and this can be attained only by the inclusion of legal norms in the data of politics and the elucidation of their meaning in research.

3. The recognition of law-as-conduct as central in political data is necessary to give relevance to political research.

4. The recognition of the place of law-as-conduct also necessitates recognition of valuation as an essential phase of political action and it facilitates the construction of significant theories of value.

5. As a result, it becomes evident that a philosophy has provided the basic ideas to guide the research, and the articulation of that philosophy may illuminate the entire enterprise.

First to be noted is that the history of political science and political theory is premised on the fact that human societies are legal organizations.[16] For Plato the enlightened legislator was not only the closest approximation to the "philosopher-king" and, therefore, the symbol of sound political problem-solving, but law, viewed principally as codes drafted by the great lawgivers, also supplied the central theme of many of his dialogues; indeed, it is the most likely clue to their synthesis.[17] From Aristotle [18] and the Stoics through the mediaeval philosophies to Locke [19] and into the nineteenth century until the specialized philosophies and social disciplines made their appearance, law was widely recognized as the distinguishing mark, the core, of the data of politics.[20] This was and is based not on indoctrination or on appreciation of the "rule of law" as the guardian of civil liberties, but on the facts and grounds discussed above, especially that law is the natural concomitant and product of social problem-solving [21] and that legal norms are central in social action.

The second implication concerns the vagueness of current political and other social science, resulting from the failure to recognize and elucidate the distinctive legal character of the data. This springs from lack of precision of the principal concepts of the discipline, such as power, decision-making, and influence. Unrelated to law, "power" is very amorphous, even when it is limited to interpersonal relations.[22]

"Decision-making," emphasized in current theories of comparative politics and comparative law,[23] is even more characteristic of daily action than are efforts to influence others. In existentialism, for example, man is viewed as making decisions every split second of the precarious, anxiety-laden exercise of his freedom. The limitation of "decision-making" to political actions still leaves a very wide notion which confuses the meaning of well-known terms without compensating advantages.[24] For example, "decision-making" is not a very suitable phrase for the creative side of legislation and adjudication. It does not suggest that there are important differences between law-making, the application of laws to specific cases, and the ministerial decisions of law-enforcing officials. It also encourages the blurring of official action with the action of the members of a society "conforming" to and deviating from rules of law and with the sanctions-process. More serious still is the ambiguity of "decision-making" in connoting, first, that it is a rational process and, then, contradicting that in concentration on the unconscious, instinctual drives, and the model of physical causation, that is, given certain forces, certain "decisions" will occur. In light of the emphasis on the latter factors, the surface implication of the rationality of decision-making disappears, leaving the most distinctive aspect of political action untouched. For the indicated reasons and those discussed above with reference to "function," "problem-solving" is a more apt inclusive term, within which "decision-making" finds an appropriate place.

Because of inherited ideas about politics, the theory of "decision-making," applied in research, has emphasized the decisions of public officials. Since their function is to solve social problems, official decision-making is obviously a datum of politics; and some of its interrelations with other aspects of the social reality of law have been discussed above. But if the premise of concentration on official decision-making is articulated, law is implied because, lacking that, there is no difference between official and nonofficial decisions. The failure to articulate the premise impairs analysis of important political problems, for example, the "legitimacy" of power, the "authority" of the officials and the public recognition of their decisions as "binding."

The relevance of research and of its products is a third problem. The failure to relate inquiry to the distinctive character of political action is bound to terminate in dubious results. For example, some of the best current studies of political parties, pressure or interest groups, the psychology of leaders, and voting stop at the threshold of what should have been their principal concern, namely, the relation of the data studied and the conclusions reached to the conduct of the officials, the laws adopted, the sanctions-process, the effect on public action, and the meaning of all this for a political philosophy.[25] However significant the search for a "behavioral unit" may be, in the absence of having discovered it and of recognizing it in narrowly defined socio-legal actions and aggregates, the current research inevitably lacks direction.

It is impossible here to support the above criticism by a detailed analysis of the indeterminateness of current research or to demonstrate the added significance which these studies would have achieved had they been focused on the social reality of law and carried through in the indicated ways. But it may be helpful, with reference to this basic problem of the subject matter of political science, to call attention to the parallel experience in criminology and to add some pertinent facts about current sociological theory.

Subjected to the same influences which motivate political and other social scientists, sustained efforts were made, especially by Garafolo and Ferri, to discover and define the "natural crime" to serve as the "behavioral unit" of criminology. This also represented a reaction against legal conceptualism and a desire to place criminology on a scientific basis. But those efforts failed because the nonlegal criteria did not define "crime" with sufficient precision and, even more, because there was a natural coincidence between criminal laws and criminal conduct—for, as anthropological research increasingly shows, customary law, at least, is not merely fortuitous or a formality. It was simply forgotten that the criminal law represents centuries-old efforts to deal with "antisocial" behavior in precise terms and that without this essential aspect of "the unit," there was no structure sufficiently articulated to deal with an infinite variety and number of data. The consequence has been that the theory of "the natural crime" has been completely abandoned. While this leaves some rather difficult problems to be dealt with, since historical accidents, vestiges, and the technicalities of advanced systems do not accord with the social reality of law, criminologists now attend carefully to the criminal law.[26] The implication for a political science which attempts to discover and define the distinctive "unit" of political data and, at the same time, ignores law is plain.

Some wider implications may be seen with reference to current sociological theory. "Social action" is a basic notion in Weber's sociology and in that of his American successors, whose analysis takes account of motivation, norms, sanctions, "values," and expectations. All of these have been analyzed in legal theory and jurisprudence, and one need only refer to treatises on criminal law to indicate the critical detail that would be available to sociologists who consulted those works regarding, for example, action, intention, recklessness, negligence, ignorance, mistake, coercion, "reasonable man," and so on. It seems obvious that theories centering on social action could be rendered much more precise if, moved by the precedent of the pioneers, especially Durkheim and Weber, legal scholarship were consulted.[27] Improvement in the precision of social theory in the above indicated ways would provide correspondingly precise guides for social research. This would be much more detailed than the relevant theory because congruent social research would take account of the particularity of the rules and how that affects the construction of socio-legal typologies and other tools of research and analysis.

It is sometimes claimed that current political research is very precise as compared, say, with Plato's *Republic* or Aristotle's *Politics*. But "precision" has no abstract or absolute value; the significance of any degree of precision depends on one's purpose. Thus, precision is meaningful in relation to knowledge, and the mere collection of a vast amount of specific data does not increase knowledge.[28] Perhaps there is some gain for some purpose in the information that 70 per cent of the voters rather than a majority of them have certain characteristics. But much more significant precision in social science is attained by the use of precise concepts, especially those which articulate the subject matter of the discipline. In sum, legal ideas provide the structure required to define social-political action and, within that field of data, to draw apt distinctions among various associations, agencies, organizations, processes, and procedures. They also demark the areas of privilege and power within which laymen and officials, political parties, interest groups, and other associations operate, while the social reality of law expresses these normative ideas and actualizes the relevant values.

Fourth, although the neglect of law is the simplest way to avoid the difficult subject of values,[29] it also omits the most significant aspect of political action. If the actualization of values in political action is ignored,[30] it is impossible to interpret what is widely recognized as the most important contribution of Western political experience—the "rule of law." [31] From Plato's *Statesman* to twentieth-century dictatorships, this has been the focal point in the quest for equality, security, and justice; and all this is incomprehensible unless the ethical significance of the "rule of law" is understood. In less striking fashion, this is true of all political action. This implies that a freely constructed legal order connotes a set of values, that is, that once law as social reality is admitted as an essential aspect of political action, so, too, is valuation.

When very abstract theories of value are applied to legal-political problems, they miss the vivid nuances of actual valuations, for example, the need to sacrifice one value to attain a more important one in that particular situation, the limitations in human resourcefulness and alternatives, and the character of valuation as experience which cannot be explained in terms of general formulas regarding the sharing of goods. The need is to narrow this gap between general theories and the actualization of values in political action. Instead of beginning with vague abstractions, the required initial approach would look in the opposite direction; law suggests an abundance of narrow concepts and typologies interrelating specific harms (delicts) and sanctions. This initial inquiry would survey and describe numerous torts, crimes, breaches of contract, violations of specific civil liberties, and so on.

From the particular values thus inferred, one could derive middle-range values: keeping promises, respecting possessions and reputations, performing services as citizens or factory owners, participating in political parties and elections, experiencing civil liberties, and so on. In this intermediate level, the significance of voluntary conduct, as contrasted with coerced or inadvertent behavior, and the affirmative meaning of bills of rights could also be elucidated. Upon this foundation of middle-range theory there could rise cogent principles culminating in general theories of valuation expressed in such ultimate concepts as "justice," "order," "equality," and "security." Interrelated in this way, the above three levels of analysis could support a realistic theory of the values of political action.

This would, finally, lead almost imperceptibly to the articulation of political philosophies which reflected relevant empirical knowledge and cogent valuation. Both phases of political action are important, but in the current situation, for reasons discussed above and elsewhere in greater detail,[32] the initial emphasis must be placed on valuation. The final emphasis, however, must be on socio-legal action. Everything else should contribute to the full understanding of that.

Social scientists, however, no less than legal scholars, are bound to be more or less specialized in their education and work; and the technicalities of modern legal systems and the vocationalism of legal education do not encourage them to emulate Durkheim, Walton Hamilton, Edwin Sutherland and Frank H. Knight. Specialization is apt to induce a sense of autonomy and, since it is also a necessity, the consequence is serious loss in the apprehension of relevant problems and in the acquisition of important knowledge. Unfortunately, no mere "addition" of the products of the various specialties can suffice. The pertinent question, moreover, is not the abandonment of valuable specialization but the cultivation of "open specialization," cognizant of the variety and range of the relevant problems and sensitive to the potential contribution of other scholars and disciplines to their solution. Accordingly, an effort was made in the above discussion to delineate the entire enterprise in which legal scholars and social scientists, especially those engaged in comparative study, participate.

No less important is recognition of the major problems of such an inquiry. For even if there is disagreement about the analysis and solutions reached, a consensus regarding which problems are the important ones would facilitate the efforts of other scholars to deal with these questions. The definite lineaments of the discipline would be more easily recognized and a sound foundation for its progress laid.

The span of a century from the beginning of modern comparative study to the present time bounds the intellectual history we must try to understand and build upon. From the vantage point of the indicated socio-legal enterprise, it is possible to enter that abundant terrain from any direction and to arrive at the same destination. If one had begun with a social science, the path would have led to legal norms and legal scholarship, just as the initial step taken above led to the social reality of law and social science.

The State's laws and its official apparatus cannot be warrantably isolated from social action. Indeed, from the viewpoint of the social scientist, the philosopher, and the intelligent layman, they are apt to be assigned a function that is merely instrumental to what goes on and what ought to be achieved in the society at large, although, actually, they also have intrinsic value. The legal comparatists who emphasized the importance of the social context and the functions of laws and institutions were constructing a bridge from the State's laws to the social reality of law. Regardless of which direction one takes in crossing that bridge, there is no escape from relating positive law, as it is traditionally conceived, to social action; and this, it is widely recognized, is "guided by" or "oriented to" legal and other norms.

A theory which brings together these various "data" into a

single meaningful configuration is, therefore, of paramount importance; in the light of such a theory, the road lies open to the interrelation or unification of presently separate social and legal disciplines and to fruitful collaboration in universities, institutes, and by informal arrangement. There is, of course, no magic in organization, and the creative tasks of scholarship remain individual ones. In any case, it seems indubitable that a scholar's work increases in significance as he comes more fully to understand his role in a large enterprise which, in the present state of human affairs, is not lacking in practical importance.

NOTES

1 Holger Pedersen, *Linguistic Science in the Nineteenth Century*, trans. John Spargo (Bloomington, Ind., 1931), 18.

2 "The comparative method is really no more characteristic of the study of language than of the other branches of modern inquiry. But it was sufficiently conspicuous in connection with the new start taken by the study early in this century to make the name of 'comparative philology,' like the earlier 'comparative anatomy' and the later 'comparative mythology,' familiar and favored, for a time, beyond any other. And the title is still accurate enough, as applied to that aspect of the study in which it is engaged in collecting and sifting its material, in order to determine correspondences and relationships and penetrate the secrets of structure and historic growth; but it is insufficient as applied to the whole study—the science of language, or linguistic science, or glottology . . . the latter makes the laws and general principles of speech its main subject, and uses particular facts rather as illustrations." William Dwight Whitney, *The Life and Growth of Language: An Outline of Linguistic Science* (New York, 1875), 315. See n. 38 *infra* for indications of the direct influence of philology on comparative law.

3 William A. Locy, *Biology and Its Makers* (New York, 1908).

4 "When we confine our attention to any one form, we are deprived of the weighty arguments derived from the nature of the affinities which connect together whole groups of organisms—their geographical distribution in past and present times, and their geological succession." Charles Darwin, *The Descent of Man* (New York, 1874), 2.

5 Myres S. McDougal, "The Comparative Study of Law for Policy Purposes: Value Clarification as an Instrument of Democratic World Order," *Am. Jour. Comp. L.*, I (1952), 24, 28–29.

6 For a similar estimate in linguistics, see Whitney, *The Life and Growth of Language*, 316.

7 ". . . the leading differences between it [the Civil Law] and the Common Law world are not differences of method or in the ways of handling source materials, but in the concepts themselves. . . ." F. H. Lawson, *A Common Lawyer Looks at the Civil Law* (Ann Arbor, Mich., 1953), 209. See also p. 45.

8 *Congrès Intn'l de Droit Comparé Tenu à Paris du 31 Juillet au 4 Août 1900, Procès-Verbaux des Séances et Documents* (Paris, 1905), I, 60 (cited hereinafter as "1900 Congress").

Pierre Arminjon, Boris Nolde, and Martin Wolff, *Traité de Droit Comparé* (Paris, 1950), I, 23, attribute this theory to De Francisci in 1921 and Kaden in 1938. See *infra* n. 10. Cf. H. C. Gutteridge, *Comparative Law* (2d ed., Cambridge, England, 1949), 5.

9 Among the first Continental writers to hold that comparative law is only a method and cannot be anything other than that was De Francisci. See *Riv. int. Filosofia del Diritto*, I (1921), 246.

10 C. J. Hamson, *The Law: Its Study and Comparison* (Cambridge, England, 1955), 21–22. René David, *Traité Elémentaire de Droit Civil Comparé* (Paris, 1950), 4, 8.

"Comparative law is nothing but a method for legal scientific research. The task of comparative law is nothing else than to compare the norms of different legal systems; it shows directly only the similarities and diversities of solutions which a particular problem has found in the different legal systems. It cannot be considered a science." Erich-Hans Kaden, "Rechtsvergleichung," *Rechtsvergleichendes HWB*, VI (Berlin, 1938), 11. Kaden refers to Stammler, Von Rauchhaupt, Koschaker, and Lautner on pp. 11–12.

So, too, A. N. Makarov, "Internationales Privatrecht und Rechtsvergleichung," *Recht und Staat*, Heft 144 (Tübingen, Germany, 1949), 5.

11 Gutteridge, *Comparative Law*, 1.

12 "Le droit comparé étant une branche du droit, sa fin est la même: régler et améliorer la conduite des hommes." Arminjon, Nolde, Wolff, *Traité*, I, 32.

13 Gutteridge, *Comparative Law*, 2, 41.

14 Quoted by Frede Castberg, *Freedom of Speech in the West* (Oslo and New York, 1960), 4.

Cf. ". . . . toute connaissance repose sur une comparaison." Novalis, quoted by K. Zweigert, "Méthodologie du droit comparé," *Mélanges Maury*, I (Paris, 1960), 580.

15 Gutteridge, *Comparative Law*, 12. For Montesquieu as founder of the sociology of law see Ehrlich, "Montesquieu and Sociological Jurisprudence," *Harv. L. Rev.*, XXIX (1916), 582, 583.

16 Gutteridge, *ibid.*, 174, 7–9. "The investigator must, first of all, ascertain how far these differences are fundamental or merely accidental; secondly, he must determine the causes underlying such differences and their relation to the general structure of the system in which they arise; and, finally, he must examine the operation of the rules in practice having regard to the legal and social environment in which each of the systems is called upon to function . . . The purpose of the comparison may be purely scientific as, for instance, when the evolution of a rule of law or of some legal institution is traced through several systems with the object of throwing light on the historical development of the same kind of rule or institution in another system" (p. 9).

17 C. J. Hamson and T. F. T. Plucknett, *The English Trial and Comparative Law* (Cambridge, England, 1952), 6, 10. Professor Hamson also

urged that legal studies be broadened, and he criticized a report on the social sciences for overlooking "the law as even an element of the social scene" (p. 7).

18 David, *Traité*, 10, 11, 15 ff., 25, and with reference to the law as a social science, 17. "We must study the history, the politics, the economics, the cultural background in literature and the arts, the religious beliefs and practices, the philosophies, if we are to reach sound conclusions as to what is and what is not common." Ferdinand F. Stone, "The End to be Served by Comparative Law," *Tulane L. Rev.*, XXV (1951), 325, 332.

19 Despite the German Imperial Ministry of Justices' remarkable *Comparative Treatise on German and Foreign Criminal Law* (1909), comparative legal scholarship was not firmly established in Germany until after the first world war. Max Rheinstein, "Comparative Law and Conflicts of Laws in Germany," *U. of Chi. L. Rev.*, II (1935), 232. Cf. Paul Koschaker, "L'histoire du droit et le droit comparé, surtout en Allemagne," *Mélanges Lambert*, I (Paris, 1938), 274, and Adolf F. Schnitzer, *Vergleichende Rechtslehre* (Basel, Switzerland, 1961), I, 17–19. Schnitzer discusses the influence of anthropology and evolution on the early German comparatists and he points out the dependence of comparative law upon the preceding contributions of natural law philosophy and the historical school, in combining their principal theses (p. 19). He then discusses the influence of nineteenth-century sociology, especially in relation to the essential requirements of a legal order (p. 20 ff.). For the present state of comparative law in Germany, see Hans G. Ficker, "L'Etat du droit comparé en Allemagne," *Rev. Int. Dr. Comp.*, X (1958), 701.

20 See pp. 17, 18, and n. 48 *infra*.

21 Ernst Rabel, *Some Major Problems of Applied Comparative Law, especially in the Conflict of Law*, a report to the Institute in the Teaching of International and Comparative Law, August, 1948, Association of American Law Schools, p. 111. He also included "systematic dogmatics." See Rheinstein, "Comparative Law and Conflicts of Laws in Germany," 246–48, for a summary of Rabel's theory of comparative law.

22 "The undoubted result of all that has been set forth is that the comparative method must be applied from a point of view very close to that of the sociology of law . . . the problem is to find equivalence in function, even though this be attained by means of different concepts. . . ." José Puig Brutau, "Realism in Comparative Law," *Am. Jour. Comp. L.*, III (1954), 49.

23 John H. Wigmore, *Harv. L. Rev.*, X (1897), 321, 389; *Harv. L. Rev.*, XI (1897), 18, 38.

24 Wigmore, "Jottings on Comparative Legal Ideas and Institutions," *Tulane L. Rev.*, VI (1931), 48, 50. By comparative law, Wigmore meant "the tracing of an identical or similar idea or institution through all or many systems . . . in short, the evolution of the idea or institution, universally considered" (p. 51).

25 *Ibid.*, 52.

26 Wigmore, "More Jottings on Comparative Legal Ideas and Institutions," *Tulane L. Rev.*, VI (1932), 264. In 1926 Wigmore had written: "Since the individual rules and institutions are bound and related together as the gross product of the social and political life of a particular race or community, their evolution cannot be fully understood without first conceiving the whole system, in its political environment and its chronology. . . ." "A New Way of Teaching Comparative Law," *Jour. Soc. Pub. Teachers L.* (1926), 7.

27 Roscoe Pound, "The Place of Procedure in Modern Law," *S. W. L. Rev.*, I (1917), 63; Pound, "What May We Expect From Comparative Law?" *ABAJ*, XXII (1936), 59.

28 Pound, "Revival of Comparative Law," *Tulane L. Rev.*, V (1930), 15, and Pound, "Introduction," *Am. Jour. Comp. L.*, I (1952), 8.

29 Rheinstein, "Teaching Comparative Law," *U. of Chi. L. Rev.*, V (1938), 617, 619, 622.

30 Rheinstein, "Teaching Tools in Comparative Law," *Am. Jour. Comp. L.*, I (1952), 98, 99. Cf. David, *Traité*, 6.

31 Hessel Yntema, "Comparative Legal Research," *Mich. L. Rev.*, LIV (1956), 899. Professor Yntema also wrote that the "more usual meaning of comparative law . . . has a universal humanistic outlook . . . like other branches of science, it contemplates that . . . the problems of justice are basically the same in time and space throughout the world" (p. 903). For his view of legal science, see Yntema, "Legal Science and Reform," *Col. L. Rev.*, XXXIV (1934), 209-10. Professor Yntema also emphasized the evaluative aspect of comparative law in "Comparative Legal Studies and the Mission of the American Law School," *La. L. Rev.*, XVII (1956-57), 545.

32 David, *Traité*, 6.

33 *Ibid.*, 5-7.

34 Thus Professor David states that the unfortunate expression "comparative law" ("droit comparé") suggests an autonomous discipline (p. 8).

35 Thurman Arnold, "The Rôle of Substantive Law and Procedure in the Legal Process," *Harv. L. Rev.*, XLV (1932), 617.

36 See, for example, *The New Systematics*, ed. Julian Huxley (Oxford, 1940), and the discussion of legal classification in Jerome Hall, *Studies in Jurisprudence and Criminal Theory* (New York, 1958), Ch. 9.

37 "In language which anticipates Montesquieu he points out the influence of geographical situation, climate and soil on the character and fortunes of nations . . . ." G. P. Gooch, *History and Historians in the Nineteenth Century* (London, 1913), 4. See Julian H. Franklin, *Jean Bodin and the Sixteenth Century Revolution in the Methodology of Law and History* (New York, 1963). Vico also merits attention in this regard. See Croce, *The Philosophy of Giambattista Vico*, trans. R. G. Collingwood (Paris, 1913), 107-10, and Giorgio del Vecchio, "La communica-

bilité du droit et les doctrines de G. B. Vico," *Mélanges Lambert*, II (Paris, 1938), 591.

38 Gustav Radbruch, "Anselme Feuerbach, Précurseur Du Droit Comparé," *Mélanges Lambert*, I (Paris, 1938), 284. "Why does the legal scholar not yet have a comparative jurisprudence? The richest source of all discoveries in every empirical science is comparison and combination. Only by manifold contrasts the contrary becomes completely clear; only by the observation of similarities and differences and the reasons for both may the peculiarity and inner nature of each thing be thoroughly established. Just as from the comparison of languages the philosophy of language, the science of linguistics itself, is produced; so from the comparison of the laws and legal customs of nations of all times and places, both the most nearly related and the most remote, is produced universal jurisprudence, the pure science of laws, which alone can infuse real and vigorous life into the specific legal science of any particular country." Feuerbach, *Kleine Schriften vermischten Inhaltes* (Berlin, 1833), 163, quoted by Harold Berman, *Ind. L. Jour.*, XXXIV (1959), 558. See Walther Hug, "The History of Comparative Law," *Harv. L. Rev.*, XLV (1932), 1054.

See Mario Sarfatti, "Les premiers pas du Droit Comparé," *Mélanges Maury*, II (Paris, 1960), 238. Lambert criticized Montesquieu for his lack of historical knowledge and sense of the continuity of evolution. 1900 Congress, 53. But cf. "Cassirer wrote pages of appreciation of Montesquieu . . . ." Hendel, "Introduction," Ernst Cassirer, *The Philosophy of Symbolic Forms, Language*, trans. Ralph Manheim (New Haven, 1953), I, 39.

39 Gutteridge, *Comparative Law*, 13.

40 Adhémar Esmein, "Le Droit comparé et l'Enseignement du Droit," 1900 Congress, I, 446.

41 Frederick Pollock, *Essays in the Law* (London, 1922), 25.

42 P. 4. In his Inaugural Lecture, delivered in October, 1888, Maitland referred to "the science of comparative jurisprudence 'if it ever exists. . . .'" Frederick Maitland, *Collected Papers* (Cambridge, England, 1911), I, 486.

43 Esmein, "Le Droit comparé," 446.

44 1900 Congress, 248, 53. The phrasing was apparently Pollock's.

45 For Comte's discussion of the comparative method, see his *Positive Philosophy*, trans. Harriet Martineau (London, 1858), 478–81. The sociology of Spencer and Gumplowicz was also influential. M. Kovalevsky, "La sociologie et l'histoire comparée du droit," 1900 Congress, I, 412.

46 Edouard Lambert, 1900 Congress, 32.

47 *Ibid.*, 35. This was in criticism of de la Grasserie's theory which is summarized *infra*, Ch. 2, n. 27.

48 *Ibid.*, 46, 35. In his *Fonction du Droit Civil Comparé* (Paris, 1903), 1–3,

914-17, Lambert had presented his view of the two types of comparative law.

49 1900 Congress, 60, 143. "According to Saleilles, the main purpose of comparative law must be to work out the improvement of municipal law. To that end one should first investigate, through a comparison with foreign laws, what ought to be the general trend of legislation, under certain social conditions. Thereby comparative law is to be distinguished from the comparative history of institutions (which is merely descriptive, and does *not* aim at *creation*, while comparative law, on the contrary, will try to determine ideal types resulting from the comparison of various legislations), as well as from sociology . . . ." Henry L. Lévy-Ullmann, "The Teaching of Comparative Law: Its Various Objectives and Present Tendencies at the University of Paris," *Jour. Soc. Pub. Teachers L.* (1925), 18. Lévy-Ullmann's "droit mondial du xx siècle" was a synthesis of Lambert's positivist theory and Saleilles' idealism. Marc Ancel, "La doctrine universaliste dans l'oeuvre de Lévy-Ullmann," *L'Oeuvre juridique de Lévy-Ullmann* (Paris, 1948), 181, 185–86. In this essay and also in his "Politique législative et droit comparé," *Mélanges Maury*, II, 9, Ancel provides excellent summaries of the history of French comparative law in the first quarter of this century, fixing its origin at the first Congress held in 1900 in Paris.

50 "The more critical school has proved that the assumption of a universal law of evolution from the simple to the complex is not invariably true with respect to culture or social institutions. It has shown that parallelisms in culture and social organization in different areas do not imply identical antecedents or necessarily bring about the same subsequent developments. Similarities may grow out of 'cultural convergencies,' proceeding from widely varied antecedents or they may be produced by imitation of a common pattern . . . Robert H. Lowie has well expressed the obituary notice of this school: . . . 'if the highest civilizations emphasize the paternal side of the family, so do many of the lowest; and the social history of any particular people cannot be reconstructed from any generally valid scheme of social evolution but only in the light of its known and probable cultural relations with neighboring peoples.' " Harry Elmer Barnes, *Historical Sociology: Its Origins and Development* (New York, 1948), 89–90.
Cf. ". . . there are *uniform tendencies* in the development of the systems proper to the various peoples, so that in general, each of them goes through successively the same phases . . . It is therefore possible (and here is one of the tasks of the Science of Universal Comparative Law) to distinguish and arrange, in a certain order, the various phases of juridical evolution in general." Del Vecchio, "The Unity of the Human Spirit as a Basis of Juridical Comparison," *Actorum Academiae Universalis Jurisprudentiae Comparativae* (Rome, 1953), III, Pars I-Pars II, 175–76.
Cf. also G. Sauser-Hall, *Fonction et méthode du droit comparé*

(Geneva, 1913), 94–95, *et passim,* and Otto Riese, "Étude sur les fonctions du droit comparé et son enseignement en Suisse," *Mélanges Guisan* (Lausanne, 1950), 181.

51 James Bryce, *Studies in History and Jurisprudence* (New York, 1901), II, 174, 187.

52 Pollock, "The History of Comparative Jurisprudence," *Essays in the Law,* 10, 12, 14.

53 *Ibid.,* 4.

54 Skepticism of the "ambitious program" of legal sociology, especially the establishment of laws of evolution, is expressed by Arminjon, Nolde, Wolff, *Traité,* I, 27–28.
   Professor Rheinstein, in 1948, at a meeting in New York, is reported to have said, "Comparative law is not a field, it is a method, it is an approach which can be used for a variety of purposes." He added: "In other years I have taught a course or seminar under the name of Sociology of Law. . . . where we have been trying to discuss the role which the social phenomenon called law is playing in society in general, not in the so-called civilized society of our present age but in past ages as well." *Institute in the Teaching of International and Comparative Law,* Association of American Law Schools, Committee on International and Foreign Law, August 31, 1948, pp. 120–21.

55 ". . . the great sociologists whose names we have just recalled [Spencer, Mill, and Comte] seldom advanced beyond vague generalities on the nature of societies, on the relations between the social and the biological realms, and on the general march of progress." Emile Durkheim, *The Rules of Sociological Method,* trans. Sarah A. Solovay and John H. Mueller (Chicago, 1938), lix.

56 Comte, *Positive Philosophy,* 474–85. Comte's contribution to logical positivism is indicated in his statement: "No proposition that is not finally reducible to the enunciation of a fact, particular or general, can offer any real and intelligible meaning" (p. 799).

57 Edward A. Freeman, *Comparative Politics* (London, 1873), iii, iv, 1, 18–19, 23. "The establishment of the Comparative Method of study," he said, "has been the greatest intellectual achievement of our time" (p. 1). "On us a new light has come. I do not for a moment hesitate to say that the discovery of the Comparative method in philology, in mythology— let me add in politics and history and the whole range of human thought —marks a stage in the progress of the human mind at least as great and memorable as the revival of Greek and Latin learning" (pp. 301–302).

58 Woodrow Wilson's *The State* (Boston, 1889) emphasized the historical and the comparative methods, and Bryce's *Modern Democracies* (New York, 1921) was viewed by its author as a pioneer application of the comparative method to the study of government. Bryce, in his Preface, referred to the "actual working" of popular governments and he "could not find that any such comparative study had been undertaken." See H. D. Lasswell, "The Comparative Method of James Bryce," *Methods*

in Social Science, ed. Stuart A. Rice (Chicago, 1931), 468. Bryce discussed "the comparative method" as a new arrival in jurisprudence, preceded by the metaphysical or a priori, the analytical and the historical methods. Bryce, *Studies in History and Jurisprudence*. See *supra* n. 51. Among the most influential works in the United States were those by John W. Burgess, *Political Science and Comparative Constitutional Law* (Boston and London, 1890–91), Frank J. Goodnow, *Comparative Administrative Law* (New York and London, 1893), and A. Lawrence Lowell, *Governments and Parties in Continental Europe* (Boston and New York, 1896).

59 "Our concern has turned away from a merely formal, legalistic and constitutional approach to a consideration of political dynamics and the processes of decision-making." Sigmund Neumann, "Comparative Politics: A Half-Century Appraisal," *Jour. of Politics*, XIX (1957), 383. Cf. David Thomson, "British Literature on Comparative Political Institutions," *Contemporary Political Science* (UNESCO, 1950), 491. But unlike the earlier evolutionary orientation, the trend has been away from the genetic motif towards the model of physical science, and "comparative politics" has become a synonym for this "political science." Karl Loewenstein, "Report on the Research Panel on Comparative Government," *Am. Pol. Sci. Rev.*, XXXVIII (1944), 541; Gunnar Heckscher, *The Study of Comparative Government and Politics* (New York, 1957), 15, 17. "The movement of which comparative studies are a vital part has been described (and descried) as behaviorism, and the quest for a universal science." William J. Siffin (ed.), *Toward the Comparative Study of Public Administration* (Bloomington, Ind., 1957), 16. Maurice Duverger, *Méthodes des Sciences Sociales* (Paris, 1961), 385.

60 Vernon Van Dyke, *Political Science: A Philosophical Analysis* (Stanford, Calif., 1960), 185.

Cf. R. H. Graveson, "The Task of Comparative Law in Common Law Systems," *Ind. L. Jour.*, XXXIV (1959), 571–90. Professor F. H. Lawson has suggested that "the differences between French and German law are much more patent and far-reaching than between English and American law." Lawson, "The Field of Comparative Law," *Juridical Rev.*, LXI (1949), 29. Kaden, "Rechtsvergleichung," 14–15, speaks of "internal" and "external" comparative law.

61 Van Dyke, *Political Science*.

62 "Of course, Boas was not against comparisons or comparative method. He wanted to improve it and specifically referred to his historical method as an improved comparative method." Oscar Lewis, "Comparisons in Cultural Anthropology," *Readings in Cross-Cultural Methodology*, ed. Frank W. Moore (New Haven, 1961), 55.

63 Regarding the ambiguity of "method" and many diverse opinions regarding its place and importance in social science, see Stuart A. Rice (ed.), *Methods in Social Science* (Chicago, 1931), 3–14.

64 John Dewey, *Logic: The Theory of Inquiry* (New York, 1938), 184.

65 "Comparative sociology is not a particular branch of sociology; it is sociology itself, in so far as it ceases to be purely descriptive and aspires to account for facts." Robert N. Bellah, "Durkheim and History," *Am. Soc. Rev.*, XXIV (1959), 452.
". . . the term comparative religion has always been awkward and unsatisfactory. It may be regarded as synonymous with the science of religion . . . ." A. Eustace Haydon, "Comparative Religion," *Ency. Soc. Sci.*, IV (1931), 131.

66 Robert M. Yerkes, "Comparative Psychology," *Ency. Soc. Sci.*, IV (1931), 129.

67 "Anthropology is the study of the similarities and the differences . . . Its data . . . are eventually seen in the perspective of similar data from various populations. In other words, the comparative perspective is as constantly dominant as is that of 'holism.'" Clyde Kluckhohn, "Common Humanity and Diverse Cultures," *The Human Meaning of the Social Sciences*, ed. D. Lerner (New York, 1959), 245–46.
". . . there is no distinctive 'comparative method' in anthropology, and the persistence of this expression has led to unnecessary confusion and artificial dichotomies . . . ." Lewis, "Comparisons in Cultural Anthropology," 55.

2.

1 See N. S. Timasheff, "Growth and Scope of Sociology of Law," *Modern Sociological Theory*, ed. H. Becker and A. Boskoff (New York, 1957), 424.

2 See references to Rheinstein *supra* nn. 29 and 30.

3 "The term science denotes a critical activity of discovery as well as the systematic knowledge founded thereon . . . Science is characterized by the method and form of its knowledge; by the control of data, formulation of generalities, and the achievement of systematic form." Victor F. Lenzen, "Philosophy of Science," *Twentieth Century Philosophy*, ed. Dagobert D. Runes (New York, 1947), 109.

4 See Karl R. Popper, "Three Views Concerning Human Knowledge," *Contemporary British Philosophy*, ed. H. D. Lewis (New York and London, 1956), 357.

5 Cf. Gustav Radbruch, *Vorschule der Rechtsphilosophie* (Göttingen, Germany, 1959), 12.

6 Roscoe Pound, "The End of Law as Developed in Legal Rules and Doctrines," *Harv. L. Rev.*, XXVII (1914), 195. Other well-known generalizations are associated with the names of Comte, Spencer, Spengler, Sorokin, and Toynbee. See Barnes, *Historical Sociology*.

7 Hall, *Theft, Law and Society* (2d ed., Indianapolis, 1952).

8 *Infra* pp. 37, 39–41, 92.

9 See Iredell Jenkins, "The Postulate of an Impoverished Reality," *Jour. of Philos.*, XXXIX (1942), 533.

10 T. M. Greene, *The Arts and the Art of Criticism* (Princeton, 1940).

11 John Dewey, *Art As Experience* (New York, 1934), 172.

12 "Like all the other symbolic forms art is not the mere reproduction of a ready-made, given reality. . . . It is not an imitation but a discovery of reality." Cassirer, *The Philosophy of Symbolic Forms, Language*, I, 53. See Ruth L. Saw, "Our Knowledge of Individuals," *Proc. Arist. Soc.* (N.S.), LII (London, 1952), 167.

"A novel about characters whose originals we have always seen about us in our daily lives may speak the truth of them and make them real or reveal their reality—as one will—in a way no practical dealings with them and no sociological analysis of them ever could do. . . . Above all, the uniqueness of a felt or perceived fact (as well as the fact of uniqueness) receives its celebration and its communication in the languages of the arts as in no other kinds of discourse." Irwin Edman, *Arts and the Man* (New York, 1939), 143. See Joyce Cary, *Art and Reality* (Cambridge, England, 1958).

13 Hugh Miller, *History and Science* (Berkeley, Calif., 1939), 128.

14 ". . . research on historical lines is one of the indispensable tools of a comparative lawyer . . . ." Gutteridge, *Comparative Law*, 28–29.

"But Caesar is comprehensible to me only because I can compare him with Alexander and Napoleon." J. Huizinga, "Historical Conceptualization," *The Varieties of History*, ed. Fritz Stern (New York, 1960), 298.

"History is movement; and movement implies comparison. That is why historians tend to express their moral judgments in words of a comparative nature like 'progressive' and 'reactionary' rather than in uncompromising absolutes like 'good' and 'bad'; these are attempts to define different societies or historical phenomena not in relation to some absolute standard, but in their relation to one another." Edward Hallett Carr, *What Is History?* (New York, 1961), 108.

15 "One of the serious errors of Collingwood's view of history . . . was to assume that the thought behind the act, which the historian was called on to investigate, was the thought of the individual actor. This is a false assumption. What the historian is called on to investigate is what lies behind the act; and to this the conscious thought or motive of the individual actor may be quite irrelevant." Carr, *ibid.*, 64–65.

Cf. Helmut Coing, "Savigny et Collingwood ou : Histoire et Interprétation du Droit," *Arch. de Philosophie du Droit* (N.S.) (1959), 1–11.

16 See Herbert Arthur Hodges, *Wilhelm Dilthey: An Introduction* (London, 1944), which includes translated selected passages; and Hodges, *The Philosophy of Wilhelm Dilthey* (London, 1952), which gives a much more detailed analysis than the earlier book.

17 John Herman Randall, Jr., *Nature and Historical Experience* (New York, 1958), 305. "What the vision *is* can only be understood by sharing it; and the many languages of the many arts, including the art of reli-

gion, are devices for communicating and sharing what has been found and seen. What the vision *means* can only be understood by relating it to other things; this is the function of interpretation, clarification, and criticism, which belongs to the humanities as disciplines; and here I would place both theology and philosophy. How the vision, the seeing and what is seen, is brought about, the devices by which the world has produced it, belong to the sciences, of nature and of man. But this is far too simple a division of labor . . . It is functions rather than disciplines that are here distinguished" (p. 304).

18 "Onto the plane of metahistory—the plane on which Spengler, Toynbee, and the other creators of all-inclusive systems have operated—almost no self-respecting historian will venture." H. Stuart Hughes, "The Historian and the Social Scientist," *Am. Hist. Rev.*, LXVI (1960), 27.

"... professional historians . . . tend to regard attempts at discovering such laws as contributions to sociology (or to some other branch of the 'generalizing' or theoretical sciences) rather than to 'history proper.' Accordingly, despite the fact that some historians undoubtedly use the evidence of the human past to establish laws of developmental change, they do not do so *qua* historians, in the opinion of most of their professional colleagues as well as on the evidence of the great bulk of historical writing. . . . See the various critical studies of Toynbee's attempt to establish such laws, *Toynbee and History*, (ed. by M. F. Ashley Montagu), Boston, 1956. The comment by A. J. P. Taylor on Toynbee's work, that 'this is not history' (p. 115), is characteristic." Ernest Nagel, *The Structure of Science* (New York, 1961), 551.

The prevailing view seems to be challenged by Professor E. H. Carr: "The historian is not really interested in the unique, but in what is general in the unique." *What is History?*, p. 80. Yet, later, Professor Carr writes: "Indeed, if I were addicted to formulating laws of history . . ." (p. 154). "History begins when men begin to think of the passage of time in terms not of natural processes—the cycle of the seasons, the human life-span—but of a series of specific events in which men are consciously involved and which they can consciously influence" (p. 178).

Cf. Huizinga, "Historical Conceptualization," 298; Louis Gottschalk, "The Historian's Use of Generalization," *The State of the Social Sciences*, ed. L. D. White (Chicago, 1956), 436; and *Generalization in the Writing of History*, ed. L. Gottschalk *et al.* (Chicago, 1963).

19 Leonard Krieger, "The Horizons of History," *Am. Hist. Rev.*, LXIII (1957), 67, 72.

20 Frederick J. E. Woodbridge, *Nature and Mind* (New York, 1937), 143.

21 See Randall, *Nature and Historical Experience*, Ch. 3.

22 See Julius Goebel, *Felony and Misdemeanor, Introduction* (New York and London, 1937); D. J. Boorstin, "Tradition and Method in Legal History," *Harv. L. Rev.*, LIV (1941), 431-32; and Boorstin, "The Humane Study of Law," *Yale L. Jour.*, LVII (1948), 970.

23 See William Dray, *Laws and Explanation in History* (London, 1957); Randall, *Nature and Historical Experience*, Ch. 3; and Susanne K. Langer, *Philosophy in a New Key* (New York, 1942), 274–75.

24 "Now, by a nongenetic science we mean a purely theoretical science; whereas a genetic science is one which understands the present in the light of the past, and supports its theoretical analysis by means of historical reconstruction." Miller, *History and Science*, 21.

25 Oliver Wendell Holmes, Jr., *The Common Law* (Boston, 1880), 1. " 'We must beware,' as Mr. Justice O. W. Holmes has said, 'of the pitfall of antiquarianism, and must remember that for our purpose our only interest in the past is for the light it throws upon the present.' . . . The legal historian must have his eye on the end of the story, and be able to pick out the beginnings of those principles and rules and institutions which have survived and are operative today." William Searle Holdsworth, *Some Lessons From Our Legal History* (New York, 1928), 6.

"Great history is written precisely when the historian's vision of the past is illuminated by insights into the problems of the present." Carr, *What is History?*, 44.

26 ". . . of course, a generalization is not much of a generalization if it applies to only two objects, but it certainly is not a statement about the unique." Gottschalk, "The Historian's Use of Generalization," 437.

27 In the 1900 Paris meeting, Raoul de la Grasserie presented a somewhat similar theory of comparative law. But his view of scientific method has been abandoned since Poincaré demonstrated the role of the hypothesis in research; and de la Grasserie's sociology of law was to include universal generalizations. De la Grasserie, "Concept général et définition de la science du droit comparé," 1900 Congress, 198, 226.

See, also, Alexandre Otetellsano, *Equisse d'une théorie générale de la Science du droit comparé* (Paris, 1940). Otetellsano's theory is that comparative law seeks similarities and differences, common principles and tendencies among present legal institutions of the same degree of civilization. Legal institutions, for him, are, for example, bank notes, checks and other negotiable instruments, law of succession, and the publicity of juridical acts to protect third persons (pp. 316–19).

28 "The jurist who approaches legal theory by way of comparative law not only becomes sceptical of facile generalizations about law, but refuses to be exclusively interested in definitions or theories which squeeze out of the law of any country the peculiarities that give it life." Lawson, Lecture delivered in 1958 at Luxembourg, International Faculty of Comparative Law, on "Comparative Law as an Instrument of Legal Culture," p. 7, which Professor Lawson kindly permitted the author to read.

29 See Arthur Lenhoff, "The Law of Evidence," *Am. Jour. of Comp. L.*, III (1954), 317, 325, 332, 340, 343; Charles Szladits, "The Concept of Specific Performance in Civil Law," *Am. Jour. of Comp. L.*, IV (1955), 233, 234; Abraham M. Hirsch, "Water Legislation in the Middle East,"

Am. Jour. of Comp. L., VIII (1959), 173, 176; and the significant sociological and legal comparisons in the study of the manor, feudalism, and marriage in Japan, France, and England by F. Joüon des Longrais, *L'Est et L'Ouest—Institutions du Japan et de L'Occident Comparées* (Tokyo, 1958), 24–25, 28–29, 101–103, 105–108, 165, 280, 333. See *infra* n. 47.

30 Professor von Mehren, after a detailed analysis of "The Type of Judicial Thinking Current in France, Germany and the United States," concludes: "The insights to be obtained by examining such variables in the equation as those considered above are relevant for a proper analysis of the problem, but they do not give a basis for definite, generalized conclusions." Arthur T. von Mehren, *The Civil Law System: Cases and Materials for the Comparative Study of Law* (Englewood Cliffs, N.J., 1957), 854.

31 I do not have in mind excellent treatises on the general problems of comparative law.

32 Durkheim, *The Elementary Forms of the Religious Life* (London and New York, 1915), 415.

33 That similarities can be generalized while differences are particular and especially important in culture is stressed by Waldemar Mitscherlich, "Des Sciences de la Nature et de l'Esprit et de leur valeur de connaissance," *Mélanges Lambert*, III (Paris, 1938), Pt. V, p. 3.

34 See *supra* pp. 29–30, 32. Cf. Miller, *History and Science*, 36, 44.

35 For example, Otetellsano, *Equisse d'une théorie générale*, 125, quotes Guillaume Duprat, *Traité de Sociologie* to the effect that sociology deals only with "abstract types." It is only knowledge of the general; and the concrete aspect of social life is essentially mobility and variety which escape scientific knowledge.

36 See Clifford R. Shaw, "Case Study Method," *Am. Sociol. Soc.*, XXI (1927), 149–57, and his studies of delinquent careers, *The Jack-Roller* (Chicago, 1931) and *The Natural History of a Delinquent Career* (Chicago, 1931). "A case study is a kind of history. It is a short-span, intensely developed, sharply focused history. It is a capsule of reality. . . . Although individual cases do not provide generalizations, they do increase knowledge. Many regard the cases as better indicators of behavior than the artificial models, working hypotheses, and quantitative measures of partial reality used by those normally called behavioralists." Emmette S. Redford, "Reflections on a Discipline," *Am. Pol. Sci. Rev.*, LV (1961), 756–57.

37 Alan F. Westin, *The Anatomy of a Constitutional Law Case* (New York, 1958). Harry M. Rosen and David H. Rosen, *But Not Next Door* (New York, 1962); Bernard Taper, *Gomillion versus Lightfoot* (New York, 1962).

38 For example, Frederic Wertham, *Dark Legend—A Study in Murder* (New York, 1944).

39 W. F. Murphy and C. H. Pritchett, *Courts, Judges, and Politics* (New York, 1961); Charles Fairman, *Mr. Justice Miller and the Supreme Court*

(Cambridge, Mass., 1939). C. H. Pritchett, *The Roosevelt Court: A Study in Judicial Politics and Values* (New York, 1948); Carl B. Swisher, *Roger B. Taney* (New York, 1935).

40 Hall, *Theft, Law and Society*, Ch. 1.

41 "The sociologist, etc., deals with his material as if the outcome were given in the known facts: he simply searches for the way in which the result was already determined in the facts. The historian, on the other hand, must always maintain towards his subject an indeterminist point of view. He must constantly put himself at a point in the past at which the known factors still seem to permit different outcomes." Huizinga, "Historical Conceptualization," 292.

42 But see Theodore Abel, "The Operation Called *Verstehen*," *Am. Jour. Soc.*, LIV (1948), 211–18. Cf. "The process of understanding is not to be identified with intuition, sudden imaginative insight or a blinding flash of illumination. . . . all understanding is, formally, the understanding of expressions . . . Expressions, as a species of physical manifestation, must be made available by observation and experiment. They must be collected, checked and classified. In this sense the social scientist uses the same methods as his colleagues in the physical sciences. . . . It is only on expressions thus elicited and collected that understanding can operate." H. P. Rickman, "The Reaction Against Positivism and Dilthey's Concept of Understanding," *Brit. Jour. Soc.*, XI (1960), 309, 310.
See also Ludwig von Mises, "Entendre et Comprendre," *Mélanges Lambert*, III, Pt. V, pp. 17, 20.

43 "It is not too difficult to state well-founded universal generalizations about social phenomena. However, such generalizations would frequently be regarded as trivial, either because they assert what is 'obvious' or because they fail to make distinctions that are held to be 'important.' For example, there appear to be no exceptions to the generalization that every religion has some form of collective ritual for renewing the common sentiments of its adherents, nor to the generalization that all delinquent children are found in societies in which there is a socially structured tension between cultural goals and institutionalized means for achieving them. The first of these is perhaps a candidate for the class of 'obvious' trivia, the second for the class of 'unimportant' ones (since it does not distinguish between types of tensions or between kinds of goals that are commonly regarded as of the greatest practical moment)." Nagel, *The Structure of Science*, 509.

44 For example, George A. Lundberg, *Foundations of Sociology* (New York, 1939).

45 Hall, *Theft, Law and Society*, Introduction.

46 Nagel, *The Structure of Science*, 505. "In short, the social sciences today possess no wide-ranging systems of explanations judged as adequate by a majority of professionally competent students . . . these contributions are primarily descriptive studies of special social facts in certain historically situated human groups, and supply no strictly universal

laws about social phenomena. . . . The possibility must certainly be admitted that nontrivial but reliably established laws about social phenomena will always have only a narrowly restricted generality" (pp. 449, 460).

47 "Comparativists . . . will have to assemble a large volume of data concerning specific solutions common to diverse legal systems before meaningful generalizations become possible. It follows that those whose eyes are fixed upon the formulation of general principles recognized by a multitude of legal systems, and who place decisive emphasis on the word 'general,' may have to wait considerable time until they will be completely satisfied by the products of comparative research." R. B. Schlesinger, "The Nature of General Principles of Law," General Report, International Acad. Comp. Law, Hamburg, 1962 (mimeo.), p. 23. See *supra* nn. 28–30 and *infra* Ch. 4, n. 9.

3.

1 For example, Kaden, "Rechtsvergleichung," *Rechtsvergleichendes HWB*, VI (1938), 13, and A. N. Makarov, "Internationales Privatrecht und Rechtsvergleichung," *Recht und Staat*, Heft 144 (Tübingen, Germany, 1949), 5.

2 "During the Congress, among all sections or committees (civil law, mercantile law, workmen's legislation, public law, etc.), it was realised that, under the diverse words, expressions, or technical forms embodying the institutions of the various countries, there is, in the civilised world, a *common groundwork of ideas and conceptions*, which, though not quite identical, draw, on certain points, so close together, as to become practically the same; like the common ground which existed, in France under the *ancien régime*, despite and above the various customs, under the name of *common law of France*, like the common ground which existed in Germany or in Switzerland previous to the establishment of unity of law in these countries; like the common ground connecting all the Anglo-Saxon legislations proceeding from English common law. To investigate into that common groundwork at once became the watchword of the Congress. The *droit commun*, defined in various ways as *droit commun législatif, droit commun contemporain, droit commun civilisé*, etc., was generally talked about." Henry L. Lévy-Ullmann, "The Teaching of Comparative Law: Its Various Objectives And Present Tendencies at the University of Paris," *Jour. Soc. Pub. Teachers L.* (1925), 19.

3 1900 Congress, 61.

4 Edouard Lambert, "Comparative Law," *Ency. Soc. Sci.*, IV (New York, 1931), 129.

5 1900 Congress, 173, 179–80.

"With the illustration of the highest points attained by juridical thought, that is to say, of the laws which are richest from a rational and humane viewpoint, this science becomes a guide to further progress and offers a kind of model for possible improvements and reforms wherever the opportunity or the need is observed. It therefore constitutes an efficient instrument for the progressive unification of the positive law of the various countries." Del Vecchio, "The Unity of the Human Spirit . . . ," *Actorum Acad. Universalis Jurisp. Comp.*, III, Pars I–Pars II (1953), 178–79. Cf. Mario Sarfatti, "Le droit comparé dans son essence et dans son application," *Mélanges Lambert*, I, 63–64; Luis Legaz y Lacambra, "Comparacion Juridica y Filosofía del Derecho," *Rev. Inst. Der. Comp. Barcelona*, I (1953), 39.

6 For example, liberation of women, socialization of tortious responsibility, transformations in property, navigation, and atomic energy. Ancel notes that these tendencies reflect the flow of universal current legislation rather than current codes. The common conceptions concern a policy underlying a sociological reality. Ancel, "Politique législative et droit comparé," *Mélanges Maury*, II, 9.

7 ". . . every comparative research has to start with the descriptive statement of the relevant legal rules or sets of rules and their similarities and dissimilarities. For this purpose we need usable common concepts, covering phenomena of the different systems that we believe to be related as different species of the same genus. We may often have to invent a new version of an old concept, a delicate but feasible operation." Ernst Rabel, *Institute in the Teaching of International and Comparative Law* (New York, 1948), prepared for Association of American Law Schools, Committee on International and Foreign Law, August, 1948, p. 111; and see Rabel, *Zeitschrift für aus. und int. Privatrecht*, I (Berlin, 1927), 17; V (Berlin, 1931), 241 ff., 282 ff.

8 Arminjon, Nolde, and Wolff, *Traité*, I, 28–30.

9 Gutteridge, *Comparative Law*, 154.

10 The "unificationist," said Gutteridge, is "an enthusiast . . . ." *ibid.*, 157; ". . . only a dream, not even a pleasant dream . . . ." Otto Riese, "Etude sur les fonctions du droit civil comparé et son enseignement en Suisse," *Mélanges Guisan* (Lausanne, 1950), 175; "a trifle naive," Philip W. Thayer, *Institute in the Teaching of Intn'l and Comp. Law*, 87.

11 ". . . almost as great a sacrifice as the abandonment of his national speech or religion." Gutteridge, *Comparative Law*, 158. Everyone agrees that it is important to distinguish the objective study of legal systems from efforts to reform them. But is it possible to keep the desire for reform from usurping the objectivity of scholarship in a field where ideals, ideologies, and traditions are extremely potent?

12 Similarly troublesome is the bias of nationality which comparatists also share with their compatriots. A striking instance is reported of Niboyet's lectures in Roumania, where he advised against adoption of German law and distortion of "la physionomie de droit roumain, qui doit savior garder son veritable usage." Otetellsano, *Equisse d'une théorie générale de la science du droit comparé*, 256. If nationality must be regarded as

a normal influence in democratic states, what obtains in dictatorial states where legal scholarship must shift with every change in political policy? Cf. Juan Hernandez Canut, "El Estudio del Derecho Comparado," *Rev. Inst. Der. Comp. Barcelona*, X (1958), 65, 71.

13 Ancel, "La doctrine universaliste dans l'oeuvre de Lévy-Ullmann," *L'Oeuvre juridique de Lévy-Ullmann* (Paris, 1948), 181, 195, 201; also Ancel, "Politique législative et droit comparé," 20; and Karl H. Neumayer, "The Role of a Uniform Legal Science in the Harmonization of the Continental Legal Systems," *Essays in Jurisprudence in Honor of Roscoe Pound*, ed. R. A. Newman (Indianapolis, 1962), 649.

14 H. H. Price, *Thinking and Experience* (London and New York, 1953), Ch. 2; C. I. Lewis, *Mind and the World-Order* (New York, 1929).

15 Ralph W. Church, *An Analysis of Resemblance* (London, 1952), 14–15; R. I. Aaron, "Our Knowledge of Universals," *Proc. Brit. Acad.*, XXXI (1945), 5.

16 "Whether there is a universal, called 'whiteness,' or whether white things are to be defined as those having a certain kind of similarity to a standard thing, say freshly fallen snow, is a question which need not concern us, and which I believe to be strictly insoluble." Bertrand Russell, *The Analysis of Mind* (New York and London, 1921), 196.

17 "It is by virtue of such a fundamental *pattern*, which all correct conceptions of the house have in common, that we can talk together about the 'same' house despite our private differences of sense-experience, feeling, and purely personal associations. *That which all adequate conceptions of an object must have in common, is the concept of the object.* The same concept is embodied in a multitude of conceptions. It is a *form* that appears in all versions of thought or imagery that can connote the object in question, a form clothed in different integuments of sensation for every different mind. Probably no two people see anything just alike . . . But if their respective conceptions of a thing (or event, or person, etc.) embody the same *concept*, they will understand each other." Langer, *Philosophy in a New Key*, 71.

18 "Nobody compares things felt to be utterly diverse . . . unless moved by some out-of-the-way interest, humorous or technical, one would not compare a salamander with a symphony, or a horse with the North Pole." Brand Blanshard, *The Nature of Thought*, I (London, 1939), 573.

19 Price, *Thinking and Experience*, 15.

20 "Indeed to distinguish and to identify are two sides of one operation . . . Clearness about likeness and clearness about difference subserve each other." Blanshard, *The Nature of Thought*, 573. See Georges Langrod, "Quelques réflexions méthodologiques sur la comparaison en science juridique," *Rev. Int. Dr. Comp.*, IX (1957), 365–68.

21 Ledger Wood, *The Analysis of Knowledge* (Princeton, N.J., 1941), 173. "Moreover, the degree of resemblance always varies inversely with the degree of difference . . ." (173).

22 Aaron, "Our Knowledge of Universals," 3.

23 Hans Kelsen, *General Theory of Law and State* (Cambridge, Mass., 1945), 4.

24 H. W. B. Joseph, *An Introduction to Logic* (2d ed., London, 1916), 31–32.

25 C. A. W. Manning, "Austin Today: Or 'The Province of Jurisprudence' Re-Examined," *Modern Theories of Law* (London, 1933), 180, 190–93.

26 Miriam T. Rooney, *Lawlessness, Law, and Sanction* (Washington, D.C., 1937), 56; *Summa Theologica of St. Thomas Aquinas*, I–II, qq. 96, 5, and I–II, 95, Art. 1; Max Weber, *Law in Economy and Society*, trans. Edward Shils and Max Rheinstein (Cambridge, Mass., 1954), e.g. pp. lxiv, lxvii, 17. Emile Durkheim, *Division of Labor in Society*, trans. George Simpson (Glencoe, Ill., 1933), 69, 94–96, 103, 111. "One of these attempts is to deny the imperative character of the legal rules by pointing to legal definitions, permissive laws, and other seemingly declarative propositions. But this is decidedly a near-sighted view of the matter. Definitions are not laws in themselves, but they are binding elements in the law, being in effect rules of interpretation that decide which of a number of possibly conflicting meanings shall be enforced. An order does not cease to be a command because it contains an explanation of what it is that is commanded. Nor is a law permitting a man to do something at his option, e.g., to dispose of his property by testament, any less a part of the system of imperatives, in this case of what we call the law of property." Morris R. Cohen, *Law and the Social Order: Essays in Legal Philosophy* (New York, 1933), 206.

27 See Eugen Ehrlich, *Fundamental Principles of the Sociology of Law*, trans. Walter L. Moll (Cambridge, Mass., 1936), 20–22, 24. Cf. *ibid.*, 62, and references to violation on 63, 73–74.

28 Ehrlich's position is unclear because he seems to support the thesis of a distinctive reaction to violation of legal norms—the *opinio necessitatis* of jurists of the continental common law. *Ibid.*, 165. "The study of 'living law' is a study of custom . . . For actual practices may be contrary to the policy of the law." Cohen, *Law and the Social Order*, 189.

29 L. I. Petrazhitsky, *Law and Morality*, trans. Hugh W. Babb (Cambridge, Mass., 1955).

30 H. L. A. Hart, *The Concept of Law* (Oxford, 1961), 24.

31 Professor Hart states that his purpose was "not to provide a definition of law," but "to advance legal theory by providing an improved analysis of the distinctive structure of a municipal legal system . . ." (p. 17). His discussion in terms of "types of law" (p. 24), "the varieties of different kinds of law to be found in a modern system such as English Law . . ." (p. 26), "important classes of law . . . ," "legal rules" (p. 27), and so on assumes that the relevant jurisprudential problems have been solved. Cf. "The method is thus primarily designed to elucidate the usual meanings of sentences. It is not a method that can demonstrate the scientific accuracy or inaccuracy or truth or falsity of statements." Graham

Hughes, "Professor Hart's Concept of Law," *Modern L. Rev.,* XXV (1962), 326.

32 For example, ". . . law without sanctions is perfectly conceivable" (p. 38).

33 *Ibid.,* 17.

34 Hall, "Legal Sanctions," *The Ethic of Power,* ed. H. D. Lasswell and Harlan Cleveland (New York, 1962), 209, and also pub. in *Natural Law Forum,* VI (1961), 119.

35 Hart, *The Concept of Law,* 27, 28.

36 See Hughes, "Professor Hart's Concept of Law," and Urban, *infra* n. 49.

37 "Power of contract is one of the two sides of freedom of contract. On one hand, freedom of contract is a freedom from restraint, an immunity from legal reprisal for making or receiving promises. On the other hand, it is not really a freedom of contract, but a power of contract, a power to secure legal sanctions when another breaks his promise. . . . This duality of freedom of contract is analyzed in 6 Corbin, Contracts § 1376 (1951)." Ian R. Macneil, "Power of Contract and Agreed Remedies," *Cornell L. Quart.* XLVII (1962), 495.

38 Hall, *Studies in Jurisprudence and Criminal Theory,* 33–37; and Hall, "Reason and Reality in Jurisprudence," *Buffalo L. Rev.,* VII (1958), 371–72.

39 Hart, *The Concept of Law,* 38–41. "There is no law prohibiting murder: There is only a law directing officials to apply certain sanctions in certain circumstances . . ." (p. 35).

40 Kelsen, *General Theory of Law and State,* 3; also, 37.

41 *Ibid.,* 61. The significance of this in legal positivism is discussed in the next chapter.

42 *Ibid.,* 45. Cf. "As ordinarily used, however, the expressions 'obeying the norm' and 'disobeying the norm' refer to the behavior of the subject. The subject can 'obey' or 'disobey' only the secondary norm" (p. 61).

43 This criticism of legal positivism must be qualified by reference to the consideration of perspectives discussed in my following chapter.

44 See Julius Stone, *The Province and Function of Law* (Cambridge, Mass., 1950), Part I.

45 Hart, *The Concept of Law,* 39.

46 Kelsen, *General Theory of Law and State,* 5.

47 *Ibid.,* 26. See the review of Hart's book by Morris Ginsberg, *Brit. Jour. Soc.,* XIII (1962), 66.

48 See Durkheim, *Division of Labor in Society.*

49 "Recurring impressions, familiarity, habit, do, indeed, breed meaning of a sort, a kind of primary intelligibility of common sense. To deny completely this intelligibility, to describe and explain, as science sometimes does, in such a way as completely to contradict the deliverances of common sense, is doubtless to court ultimate unintelligibility. Yet for science and philosophy alike this primary intelligibility, as we may, perhaps,

call it, leaves much to be desired." Wilbur Marshall Urban, *The Intelligible World* (New York, 1929), 180.

50 Joseph H. Beale, *A Treatise on the Conflict of Laws* (New York, 1935), I, 47–48, reprinted in Hall, *Readings in Jurisprudence* (Indianapolis, 1938), 415.

51 Ralph W. Church, *An Analysis of Resemblance* (London, 1952), 95–96, 102. See *infra* pp. 98, 99, 101, 103.

52 This has been urged by well-known comparatists who are very familiar with the structure of the foreign system. "The only way to understand the Civil Law systems is to go inside them and learn their tunes . . . ." F. H. Lawson, *A Common Lawyer Looks at the Civil Law,* 210. Professor David suggests that it is necessary that the student of foreign law place himself as fully as possible in the situation of the jurist of that system. *Traité,* 9–10. The writer's experience in his seminar in Criminal Law at the University of Freiburg, Germany, 1961, in collaboration with Professor H. H. Jescheck, confirms the opinions of these distinguished comparatists.

53 Arminjon, Nolde, and Wolff, *Traité,* I, 29.

54 L. Susan Stebbing, *A Modern Introduction to Logic* (London, 1933), 389.

55 H. H. Jescheck, *Entwicklung, Aufgaben und Methoden der Strafrechtsvergleichung. Antrittsrede* (Tübingen, Germany, 1955), 38.

56 R. B. Schlesinger, "The Common Core of Legal Systems—An Emergent Subject of Comparative Study," *XXth Century Comparative and Conflicts Laws, Legal Essays in Honor of Hessel E. Yntema* (Leyden, 1961), 73.

57 *Ibid.,* 76. An American scholar trained in a classification which includes law and equity, torts, wills, sales, and evidence would need to be sufficiently familiar with Continental law to be able to locate the corresponding rules there, since their classifications are constructed on different lines. See Charles Szladits, *Guide to Foreign Legal Materials: French, German, Swiss* (New York, 1959), 515–21.

58 The ambiguity of "legal theory" needs to be resolved if precision is desired. This requires not only the abandonment of popular uses of "theory" but also the distinction of legal theory from jurisprudence. The suggested criterion is the level of generalization. The usual interpretation of words by lawyers and judges is distinguished from legal theory which provides a system of ideas relevant to that interpretation. Such theory is, in turn, distinguishable from theorizing about all law, which is the province of jurisprudence. Inserted between theory and jurisprudence is "transnational theory" which generalizes what is common to a particular branch of two or more national systems but falls short of universal generalization regarding all law. See Hall, *Studies in Jurisprudence and Criminal Theory,* Ch. 1. Professor Otto Brusiin has suggested "metatheory." But since this "does not—like legal theory—analyze the legal phenomena but the propositions made by legal theorists

about legal phenomena," it is necessary to distinguish this from "transnational theory." Brusiin, "International Aspects of Legal Theory," *Estudios Juridice-Sociales, Homenaje al Legaz y Lacambra* (Santiago, Spain, 1960), 247.

59 Hall, *General Principles of Criminal Law* (2d ed., Indianapolis, 1960), Ch. 1. A translation of this chapter by Dr. Joachim Herrmann, entitled "Strafrechtstheorie" was published in *Zeitschrift für die gesamte Strafrechtswissenschaft,* 73 Band Heft 3 (Berlin, 1962), 385. The theory is summarized in Hall, "The Scientific and Humane Study of Criminal Law," *Boston U. L. Rev.,* XLII (1962), 267–73.

60 For civilian readers, it should be noted that "doctrine," as used here, means certain propositions of intermediate generality, examples of which follow immediately in the text.

61 Cf. Wilhelm Sauer, *Allgemeine Strafrechtslehre* (2d ed., Berlin, 1949).

62 Gutteridge, *Comparative Law,* 61.

63 Cf. Schlesinger, "The Common Core of Legal Systems," 79.

64 See *infra* Ch. 5, n. 51.

65 Castberg, *Freedom of Speech in the West.*

66 See Seve Ljungman, "The Unification of Scandinavian Law," *Egyptian Society of International Law* (Cairo, 1959), 37.

67 For a discussion of this last and other such differences see Felix Weiser, *Trusts on the Continent of Europe* (London, 1936), 11 ff.

68 1900 Congress, 30–31, 53–54. He had the strong support of Saleilles, both as regards the two types of comparative law and the objective of the ancient one—to derive the concepts common to different legal systems. Lambert was rather diffident regarding the sociology of law, stating he was not qualified to say how it should be taught (p. 54).

69 *Ibid.,* 60.

70 "In general, comparative law will have most difficulty in forcing entry where law teaching is not presented in a framework of economics and political science; for comparative jurisprudence and law as a social science are two aspects of the same thing." Lambert, "Comparative Law," *Ency. Soc. Sci.,* IV (1931), 129.

71 To this effect see Schnitzer, *Vergleichende Rechtslehre,* I, 32, where the author maintains that legal comparatists should study legal institutions to determine whether they are "living law" or whether certain provisions in the codes are only "dead letters." Comparative study, he holds, must deal with the reality of law.

4.

1 "Metaphysics has always been a striving after ultimate synthesis, as opposed to what Berkeley called minute philosophies." Morris R. Cohen, *A Preface to Logic* (New York, 1944), 64.

Every legal philosophy deals to some extent and in one way or another with the logic of law, the value of it, if only to exclude that from the province of law, and at least those relations to fact needed to give meaning to the concepts, establish "efficacy," and so on, indicating that jurisprudence is involved in every subject-matter discussed in philosophy. It is, therefore, more difficult to say in what respects legal philosophy differs from "general" philosophy than it is to point out the similarities. Certainly, the frequent assertion that jurisprudence is only a branch or application of philosophy is not supported by reference to the great philosophers whose complete work is known, prior to the modern age of specialization when philosophy became departmentalized (much of Aristotle's contribution to jurisprudence, including Theophrastus' work, is lost). For that shows plainly that thinking about law was integral to, and often central in, their philosophy. Not only is the usual description of legal philosophy as an "application" of philosophy misleading but, also, if the central purpose of philosophy is "ultimate synthesis," some legal philosophies approximate that more closely than do many specialties taught in departments of philosophy.

2 Hall, "Plato's Legal Philosophy," *Studies in Jurisprudence and Criminal Theory*, Ch. 3.

3 "The laws restricting liberty, the racial laws, in general the fascist laws that had violated certain fundamental principles on which the liberal state was based, had raised anew the old question: must the citizen obey unjust laws?" Norberto Bobbio, "Trends in Italian Legal Theory," *Am. Jour. Comp. L.*, VIII (1959), 330.

4 "An anthropological approach to law is flatly behavioristic and empirical in that we understand all human law to reside in human behavior and to be discernible through objective and accurate observation of what men do in relation to each other and the natural forces that impinge upon them." E. Adamson Hoebel, *The Law of Primitive Man* (Cambridge, Mass., 1954), 5.

5 The relevant literature from Maine to the present is voluminous. In a recent work, there is apt reference to "the characteristic ethos and way of life of the people . . . the present customary law, which reflects, *par excellence*, the people's own choice of legal system . . . the daily practice of the people, and the normative rules founded on such practice and enforced by their courts. Discovery of such rules is to a large extent by a process of observation and analysis of what has been observed . . . ." A. N. Allott, "The Study of African Law," *Sudan L. Jour. and Rep.* (1958), 258.

6 "As devotees of freedom, we must accept the fact that order is a necessity, freedom a comparative luxury. And as regards the legal order, it is unanimity that is imperative; if free agreement is not reached, it must be imposed, or chaos will ensue." Frank H. Knight, "Science, Society, and the Modes of Law," *The State of the Social Sciences*, ed. Leonard D. White (Chicago, 1956), 11. See the collection of essays in Carl Friedrich (ed.), *Authority* (Cambridge, Mass., 1958).

7 "As observed by Mr. Bentham, the provisions of different systems are never precisely alike; the only parts in which they agree exactly, being those leading expressions which denote the necessary parts of every system of law." John Austin, *Lectures on Jurisprudence* (4th ed., London, 1879), II, 1108, n. 54 (2).

8 Gutteridge, *Comparative Law*, 16; Otto Brusiin, "Methodological Aspects of Legal Theory," *Studi in onore di Emilio Betti* (Milan, 1960), 6, n. 6. See the criticism of positivism by M. Ancel, "Valeur Actuelle des Etudes de Droit Comparé," *20th Century Comparative and Conflicts Law—Legal Essays in Honor of Hessel E. Yntema*, 21–22.

9 "So, juridical comparison presupposes the idea of Law, though it neither contemplates this idea *sub specie aeterni*, nor analyses it in the abstract, but considers it in the concrete, in its manifold realizations as an element or fact of experience." Del Vecchio, "The Unity of the Human Spirit . . . ," *Actorum Acad. Universalis Jurisp. Comp.*, III, Pars I-Pars II (1953), 173–74. See Lawson, *supra* n. 28, Ch. 2.

10 This direction of thought has its origin in some of Plato's dialogues (where he speaks of "participation") and especially in Aristotle's theory of universals. It was elaborated by Hegel and post-Hegelian social scientists, notably Dilthey, who had read William James. Currently on the Continent, Scheler's and Hartmann's theory emphasizes the actualization of values in conduct. Wilhelm Sauer has incorporated some of these insights into his legal philosophy. But much more has been achieved in that direction in Latin America, especially in the work of Carlos Cossio, Miguel Reale, and Luis Recaséns Siches. See *Latin-American Legal Philosophy*, "20th Century Legal Philosophy Series," (Cambridge, Mass., 1948), III; Cossio, "Jurisprudence and the Sociology of Law," *Col. L. Rev.*, LII (1952), 356; Hall, "Integrative Jurisprudence," *Interpretations of Modern Legal Philosophies—Essays in Honor of Roscoe Pound*, ed. Paul L. Sayre (New York, 1947), 313, revised as Ch. 2 of Hall, *Studies in Jurisprudence and Criminal Theory;* Hall, *Living Law of Democratic Society* (Indianapolis, 1949), Ch. 3; and Hall, "Reason and Reality in Jurisprudence," *Buffalo L. Rev.*, VII (1958), 351 ff., trans. as *Razon Y Realidad en el Derecho*, trans. P. David (Buenos Aires, 1959); *Mélanges Dabin*, I (Paris, 1963), 101–25; and M. J. Sethna (ed.), *Contributions to Synthetic Jurisprudence* (Bombay, 1962).

11 "It is not the principle in the books, but the principle in action, that is truly law . . . ." Roscoe Pound, "The Place of Procedure in Modern Law," *S. W. L. Rev.*, I (1917), 60. "But law is more than rules; it is a process of living." E. Borchard, "Rapport," *Actorum Acad. Universalis Jurisp. Comp.*, II (1) (Rome, 1934), 402. "Aux yeux du juriste comparatif, le droit est un phénomène naturel régi par les lois naturelles." Arminjon, Nolde, Wolff, *Traité*, I, 27. "One needs, however, the wherewithal not only to distinguish the behavior aspects ["law-ways"] (along

with the relevant attitudes) from the Rules of Law, but the wherewithal to lump the two, and to include in the reference such other things as tribunals, or specialized law-personnel." K. N. Llewellyn, "The Normative, The Legal, and the Law-Jobs: The Problem of Juristic Method," *Yale L. Jour.*, XLIX (1940), 1358.

12 "All the social sciences study human activity . . . The elimination of disorder is the principal task of social control . . . jurisprudence as a social science . . . is concerned with . . . not law, as such, but human behavior as influenced by, or in relation to, the social factor of disorder." Huntington Cairns, *The Theory of Legal Science* (Chapel Hill, 1941), 1, 2, 9.

13 John C. Gray, *The Nature and Sources of the Law* (2d ed., New York, 1927), 89–92. "If the Law of the State be seen as in first essence not a 'code' nor a body of Rules, but as in first essence a going institution, it opens itself at once to inquiry by the non-technician. Like any other institution, it will have purposes, it will be serving needs; it will consist in good part of interlocking organized activities, it will have precipitated certain specialized crafts, followed by specialists; it will have developed an ideology which is a necessary part of itself." K. N. Llewellyn, "The Normative, the Legal, and the Law-Jobs," "Foreword" (in the reprint).

14 "So thoroughly have norms become a part of the human mode of existence that they are to a high degree internalized. For the individual growing up in a society each norm is not necessarily an external rule which he may obey or try to evade; it may be a part of himself not regarded objectively at all or understood and felt as a rule, but simply a part of himself automatically expressed in behavior. Such internalized norms guide and determine his intuitive judgments of others and his intuitive judgments of himself. They lead to the phenomena of conscience, of guilt feelings, of striving, of elation and depression. They are more personal than habit, deeper than consciousness." Kingsley Davis, *Human Society* (Minneapolis, 1948), 55. See Theodore M. Newcomb, *Social Psychology* (New York, 1950), 305, 309.

15 "If interlocking behavior gets patterned in fact, with a resulting back-and-forth of adjusted action and adjusted expectation, deviations will bother; generalizable pictures of rightness and of rights are pretty well bound to result. This does not depend on anybody wanting such patterns to develop, or planning them, or preaching them, though any or all of these things may happen. It does not even depend on people knowing that they have fallen into behaving along such patterned, interlocking lines, or that they have fallen into patterns of action and attitude which 'strain' toward some particular line of normatizing." Llewellyn, "The Normative, the Legal, and the Law-Jobs," 1360.

16 ". . . in the history of the human race, organic response is prior to judgment in the development of speech. Our consciousness of meaning is, for the most part, a development of the consciousness of our organic attitudes or 'sets' toward other objects. Much can be said for the view

that an act of judgment is necessarily involved in apprehending the meaning of any proposition. But we must not confuse the meaning of a proposition with our conscious apprehension of that meaning." Cohen, *A Preface to Logic*, 28.

17 "It has been asked, as we noticed above, is a concept merely an object of thought, with no existence in things (as it is put, outside our minds)? or does it exist in things? . . . Concepts, we maintained, have existence in things, as well as in our minds. The thing which I can pull out of my pocket, and see and feel, and hear ticking, is itself a machine wherein the movement of wheels causes hands to tell the time of day as set forth in stating the concept of a timepiece. What I conceive a timepiece to be, that (if my concept is a right concept) every particular timepiece is; what I know about things is the nature of the things; nor would it otherwise be they wherewith my knowledge dealt . . . ." H. W. B. Joseph, *An Introduction to Logic*, 70.

18 ". . . the concept of law will be defined as an order which depends upon an enforcement *staff*." Weber, *Law in Economy and Society*, 6. The sociologist studies conduct "oriented" to those norms. For example: "In actual life, conduct may be oriented toward an order . . ." (pp. 3–4). "The thief orients his conduct towards the validity of the criminal law, viz., by trying to conceal it . . . One who engages in a duel orients his conduct toward the honor code . . ." (p. 4). "An order will be called *law* if it is externally guaranteed by the probability that coercion (physical or psychological), to bring about conformity or avenge violation, will be applied by a *staff* of people holding themselves specially ready for that purpose" (p. 5).

19 "But though the features of things exist in the things, besides being conceived by our minds, the manner of their existence is different in an important respect from that of our conceiving them. In our minds, each is to some extent isolated; my knowledge of an individual thing is expressed piecemeal in many predicates about it; each predicate expressing a different concept, or a different feature in the nature of the thing. But in the thing these features are not isolated. The individual thing is at once and together all that can be predicated of it separately and successively . . . ." Joseph, *An Introduction to Logic*, 70.

20 "The prevalent trend is to regard law as positive enactment rather than a body of principles inherent in social conduct . . . Hence, law is identified with legislation and is attributed to the legislative organ by which it is enacted, rather than to the infinitely diversified social structure by which law is required. The tendency therefore is to simplify legal theory by differentiating law from the facts of life, by personalizing the legal process in terms of the agencies by which it is conducted, rather than as a function of the needs of human beings whom they are supposed to serve." Hessel E. Yntema, "Comparative Legal Studies and the Mission of the American Law School," *La. L. Rev.*, XVII (1956–57), 542, 544.

21 Nicolai Hartmann, *Ethics*, trans. Stanton Coit (London and New York, 1932).

22 See Charles S. Hyneman, *The Study of Politics—The Present State of American Political Science* (Urbana, Ill., 1959, reprinted 1961), 44–45 and *infra* Ch. 6, nn. 9–11.

23 "From this primary legal order the rule of law is derived by jurists and legislators by very intricate processes which I endeavored to expound in the Sociology of Law. The rule of law cannot be understood sociologically without considering the legal order from which it arises." Eugen Ehrlich, "Montesquieu and Sociological Jurisprudence," *Harv. L. Rev.*, XXIX (1915–16), 584.

24 A recent American book, Julius Cohen, R. A. H. Robson, and A. Bates, *Parental Authority: The Community and the Law* (New Brunswick, N.J., 1958), compared rules of law concerning the control of minors with relevant public attitudes. This writer studied public opinion in England in the eighteenth and nineteenth centuries in relation to the law of theft (*Theft, Law and Society*, Indianapolis, 1952). And, of course, A. V. Dicey's *Law and Opinion in England During the Nineteenth Century* (London and New York, 1905; 2d ed., 1914) has long been a classic in this field. The relevant list could no doubt be considerably amplified, but the fact remains that studies of this subject which meet current standards of social research are rare.

5.

1 Julian Huxley, "The Uniqueness of Man," *Yale Review*, XXVIII (1939), 475, 476, 491, 500.

2 Siegfried F. Nadel, *The Theory of Social Structure* (Glencoe, Ill., 1957). Nadel emphasizes differential command of other persons' actions and over benefits and resources. Robert K. Merton, *Social Theory and Social Structure* (Glencoe, Ill., 1957); Talcott Parsons, "The Social Structure of the Family," *The Family: Its Function and Destiny*, ed. R. N. Anshen (New York, 1959), 241. Morris Ginsberg, "The Problems and Methods of Sociology," *The Study of Society*, ed. F. C. Bartlett, *et al.* (London, 1946), 443–50; Robert Bierstedt, *The Social Order: An Introduction to Sociology* (New York, 1957); and Kingsley Davis, *Human Society*. For a very critical essay on current sociological theories of structure, see Georges Gurvitch, "Le Concept de Structure Sociale," *Cahiers Internationaux de Sociologie*, XIX (Paris, 1955), 3.

See the survey article by W. J. McEwen, "Forms and Problems of Validation in Social Anthropology," *Current Anthropology* IV (1963), 155.

Gabriel A. Almond, "Comparative Political Systems," *Jour. of Politics*, XVIII (1956), 391, reprinted in *Political Behavior*, ed. H. Eulau, S. J. Eldersveld, and M. Janowitz (Glencoe, Ill., 1956), 34.

3 "A status, in the abstract, is a position in a particular pattern [of social behavior] . . . A status, as distinct from the status of the individual who may occupy it, is simply a collection of rights and duties. . . . When he puts the rights and duties which constitute the status into effect, he is performing a role. Role and status are quite inseparable. . . ." R. Linton, *The Study of Man* (New York and London, 1936), 113–14.

4 Continuing, he states: "The family, the state, the church, the political party, the business firm, the occupational union, the school and college, the scientific, artistic, philanthropic, or other society, the army and the navy, even an organized criminal gang are but the objectification and materialization of the respective law-norms and law-convictions of their members." Pitirim Sorokin, *Society, Culture, and Personality* (New York, 1947), 77.

5 "When we talk about what people do in society we are interested, as sociologists, not in their behavior as such, for this is the subject of the science of social psychology, but rather in the type of behavior that is considered socially acceptable or unacceptable. . . . the norms are of particular interest to sociology because they constitute the basis, the very foundation, of social organization. It is the norms that contribute order and stability to human societies." Bierstedt, *The Social Order*, 140,171. According to Bierstedt, the norms include "laws, statutes, rules, regulations, customs, folkways, mores, taboos, fashion, rites, rituals, ceremonies, conventions, etiquette" (p. 178). Cf. ". . . the totality of folkways, mores, and laws in a society are related in a systematic fashion and that consequently a fruitful approach to understanding social structure is in terms of the normative system." Davis, *Human Society*, 70.

6 Sorokin, *Society, Culture, and Personality*, 41–65.

7 See Llewellyn, Ch. 4, nn. 11 and 13.

8 "An institution can be defined as a *set* of interwoven folkways, mores, and laws built around one or more functions. It is a part of the **social** structure, set off by the closeness of its organization and by the distinctness of its functions." Davis, *Human Society*, 71. Cf. the theory of M. Hauriou, and G. Renard, *La Théorie de l'Institution* (Paris, 1930).

9 Hall, Ch. 3, n. 34. See also *infra* n. 11 and Ch. 4, n. 18.

10 "The Plains military societies had the power to punish members who failed in their duties to the society. Secret societies of Africa and Melanesia may destroy members who reveal their secrets to the non-initiate." E. A. Hoebel, "Primitive Law and Modern," *Transactions of the New York Academy of Sciences*, Series II, V (New York, 1942), 40.

11 The position held by Weber, Sorokin, and other sociologists is that there is no important difference between the laws of the State and those of various subgroups. See Weber, *Law in Economy and Society*, 6, 17, and *supra* n. 9.

12 Sumner's classical division of norms into mores and folkways has been criticized by Sorokin, who prefers: law-norms, technical norms, fashion

and etiquette, and an uncertain omnibus category. Sorokin, *Society, Culture, and Personality*, 87. A more detailed classification of norms is that of Richard T. Morris, "A Typology of Norms," *Am. Soc. Rev.*, XXI (1956), 610. Professor Morris' principal categories are I, Distribution of Norm, II, Mode of Enforcement, III, Transmission, and IV, Conformity; and each of these is subdivided into several types. Class II does not, however, include such distinctions among sanctions as penal, restitutive, preventive, and correctional.

13 See, generally, Luis Recaséns Siches, "Les usages sociaux et leur différenciation d'avec les normes juridiques," *Droit, Morale, Moeurs* (Paris, 1936), 145.

14 See Richard Arens and Harold D. Lasswell, *In Defense of Public Order —The Emerging Field of Sanction Law* (New York, 1961), 171–97.

15 For a critical, suggestive discussion, see Clyde Kluckhohn, "Values and Value-Orientations in the Theory of Action," *Towards a General Theory of Action*, ed. T. Parsons and E. A. Shils (Cambridge, Mass., 1951), 388. Values, abstracted from action, are individual or commonly shared conceptions of desirables, that is, they are connected with approval and disapproval. Values are classified by their "dimensions" in terms of modality, content, intent, generality, intensity, explicitness, extent, and organization. Like Petrazhitsky, Kluckhohn holds that values ("ethical impulsions") have only a subject while norms ("legal impulsions") are bilateral.

16 Hall, *Living Law of Democratic Society*, Ch. 2.

17 "It is true that we meet everywhere with what the systematist regards as 'difficult' groups. In almost every Class, Order, and family, even in many genera, by the side of well-marked and clearly definable species there is a residue in which the limits of species seem to become blurred. . . . What is significant is the very general discontinuity of species and the readiness with which most of them fall, almost as it were of themselves, into definable genera and categories of higher order." W. T. Calman, "A Museum Zoologist's View of Taxonomy," *The New Systematics*, ed. Julian Huxley, 456.

18 *Traité*, I, 42–53.

19 *Ibid.*, 48, 39.

20 Hall, "Culture, Comparative Law and Jurisprudence," *Studies in Jurisprudence and Criminal Theory*, Ch. 6.

21 David, *Traité*, 224–26.

22 David, "Existe-t-il un droit occidental?" *XXth Century Comparative and Conflicts Law—Legal Essays in Honor of Hessel E. Yntema* (Leyden, 1961), 56.

23 For an excellent critique, see Edgar Bodenheimer, "Reflections on the Rule of Law," *Utah L. Rev.*, VIII (1962), 1; see *infra* n. 49. Hall, *General Principles of Criminal Law*, 48–68.

24 F. H. Lawson, "A New Book on French Law" (R. David, *Le Droit Français*, Paris, 1960), *Jour. Soc. Pub. Teachers L.*, VI (1961), 133–34.

See André Tunc and Suzanne Tunc, *Le droit des États-Unis d'Amérique —Sources et techniques* (Paris, 1955), 174–84.

25 Vivian Bose, "Legal Education as a Basis for the Rule of Law in Africa and Eastern Countries," *Col. Univ. L. Alum. Bul.*, VII (1962), 2.

26 As noted, in his later article, M. David emphasized the "rule of law," but for the reason indicated above, this seems to imply the wider notion stated here. Cf. "If we identify the Rule of Law with government according to rules and regulations, the concept becomes drained of the ingredients of value which are normally associated with it. . . . There can be a despotism of rules as well as a despotism of individual whim." Bodenheimer, "Reflections on the Rule of Law," 4.

27 See Ralph J. D. Braibanti, "Comments on the Seminar Report," *Am. Pol. Sci. Rev.*, XLVII (1953), 666–69.

28 See, for example, Geoffrey Barraclough, *History in a Changing World* (Oxford, 1956).

29 Max Beloff, *Europe and the Europeans* (London, 1957).

30 1900 Congress, 438. ". . . des types juridiques distincts" (p. 440). The early social types were constructed with a view to genetic explanation. For a survey, see S. R. Steinmetz, "A Classification of Social Types and a Catalogue of Peoples," *Formative Influences of Legal Development*, ed. A. Kocourek and J. H. Wigmore (Boston, 1918), 3.

31 Hall, *Studies in Jurisprudence and Criminal Theory*, 52–70.

32 Hodges, *The Philosophy of Wilhelm Dilthey*. For William James' influence on Dilthey, see *ibid.*, xxi, 204.

33 "By far the greater part of taxonomy is based on morphology . . . Classification is a *sine qua non* of any biological research . . . ." W. B. Turrill, "Experimental and Synthetic Plant Taxonomy," *The New Systematics*, ed. Huxley, 47.

34 "The evolution of the ideal type in sociology was determined by the attempts to transform comparative method into a more precise procedure. . . . Sociology arose in the nineteenth century with the attempt to combine an organismic concept of society with a positivism of procedure. Its basic theory was evolutionary; its materials were historical; its method was comparative." Don Martindale, "Sociological Theory and the Ideal Type," *Symposium on Sociological Theory*, ed. Llewellyn Gross (Evanston, Ill., 1959), 59.

35 Carl G. Hempel, "Problems of Concept and Theory Formation in the Social Sciences," *Science, Language, and Human Rights* (Philadelphia, 1952), 67.
"The concept of 'pattern' must be distinguished from the neighboring concept of 'type.' The type may be called a 'logical' pattern or the pattern an 'ontological' type." Florian Znaniecki, *Social Actions* (New York, 1936), 37.

36 Some interesting applications of "typology" may be seen in Salvador de Madariaga's *Englishmen, Frenchmen, Spaniards* (London, 1931) where the thesis is that the predominant tendency in the Englishman is

action, that of the Frenchman, thought, and that of the Spaniard, passion. Madariaga recognizes that the three tendencies are found in all men, but his thesis is that one or the other tendency predominates.

37 See Arnold Brecht, *Political Theory* (Princeton, N.J., 1959), 43–46, 108–12. Unless the criteria constituting the extreme types are definitely articulated with the greatest possible precision, the flow of the data becomes unmanageable and the intended meanings are confused. Hempel, "Problems of Concept and Theory Formation . . . ," 68.

38 Hall, *Studies in Jurisprudence and Criminal Theory*, 54–55.

39 "Since, moreover, social phenomena evidently escape the control of the experimenter, the comparative method is the only one suited to sociology." Durkheim, *The Rules of Sociological Method*, 80–81, 125. "He therefore criticises those sociologists and anthropologists who understand the comparative method to consist in the indiscriminate collection of facts and who believe that the sheer weight of documentation can prove anything. Durkheim, rather, insists that comparison can only be meaningful when the facts compared have been carefully classified in terms of a systematic and theoretically relevant typology. This means for him especially the typological classification of whole societies or what he calls 'social species.' . . . The arrangement of social types or species shows a rough sequence, in that the more complex types emerge from the simpler. But there is no suggestion of 'inevitable stages': the genetic concept was not tainted with unilinear evolutionism." Robert N. Bellah, "Durkheim and History," *Am. Soc. Rev.*, XXIV (1959), 451.

40 See Bellah, *infra* n. 45.

41 See, for example, Weber, *The Methodology of the Social Sciences*, trans. Edward A. Shils and Henry A. Finch (Glencoe, Ill., 1949), 89–94; and Weber, *Law in Economy and Society*, xxxv–xliii, *passim*.

42 "An ideal type is formed by the one-sided *accentuation* of one or more points of view and by the synthesis of a great many diffuse, discrete, more or less present and occasionally absent *concrete individual* phenomena, which are arranged according to those one-sidedly emphasized viewpoints into a unified analytical construct. In its conceptual purity, this mental construct cannot be found anywhere in reality." Weber, *The Methodology*, 90.

43 J. W. N. Watkins, "Ideal Types and Historical Explanation," *Readings in the Philosophy of Science*, ed. Herbert Feigl and May Brodbeck (New York, 1953), 723.

44 See B. F. Hoselitz, "On Comparative History," *World Politics*, IX (1957), 267; Martindale, "Sociological Theory and the Ideal Type."

45 Carlo Antoni, *From History to Sociology: The Transition in German Historical Thinking*, trans. Hayden V. White (Detroit, 1959), 181–83. "A satisfactory typology of societies remains to be achieved, though it is one of the first tasks of sociology as Durkheim clearly saw. All comparative work which does not use at least an implicit typology is severely limited. This stricture applies to at least some of the cross-

cultural survey studies which use, say, '400 societies,' but where we have no idea how comparable these societies in fact are in terms of structural types. . . . It is in the work of Max Weber rather than Durkheim that the most fruitful beginnings of a satisfactory typology are to be found." Bellah, "Durkheim and History," 451. Talcott Parsons criticizes "ideal types" as concentration on extreme situations and therefore incompatible with equilibrium-analysis and the formation of a general theory. Parsons, *Essays in Sociological Theory, Pure and Applied* (Glencoe, Ill., 1949), 91. See also J. R. Schumpeter, "Capitalism," *Ency., Brit.*, IV (1958), 801–807. "It must also be assumed, however, that ideal types will continue to be employed as long as sociology or any science relies upon the comparative method." Martindale, *ibid.*, 88.

For further difficulties involved in dealing with such large types as "totalitarianism," "fascism," and "mass-movement regime," see Robert C. Tucker, "Towards a Comparative Politics of Movement-Regimes," *Am. Pol. Sci. Rev.*, LV (1961), 281. According to Tucker's typology, Lenin's regime was not totalitarian, while Stalin's was totalitarian and fascist but not communist. This is criticized by Peter Wiles, "Comment on Tucker's Movement-Regimes," *ibid.*, 290.

46 "Six criteria are proposed [by Kroeber] . . . 'To the student of culture, civilizations are segregated or delimited from one another by no single criterion: partly by geography, partly by period, partly by speech, religion, government, less by technology; most of all, probably, by those activities of civilization that are especially concerned with values and the manifest qualities of style.' " David Mandelbaum, "The Study of Complex Civilizations," *Current Anthropology: A Supplement to Anthropology Today*, ed. W. L. Thomas, Jr. (Chicago, 1956), 205. "However much all of us, like Lowie, champion the comparative method, in this field we have as yet little material for making effective comparisons. . . . Anthropologists' insistence on the comparative method would come with better grace if that method were clarified, lucid examples given, its limitations defined" (p. 221).

47 "There is no universal general African law; there are rather a limited number of *types* of legal features, attitudes and procedures. On the basis of these types, it is possible to construct a *typology of African law* . . . ." Antony Allott, *Essays in African Law* (London, 1960), 64.

48 See *supra* Ch. 3 text, at notes 58–60.

49 Samuel I. Shuman, "Philosophy and the Concept of Judicial Independence," *Wayne L. Rev.*, VIII (1962), 363. Professor Stefan Rozmaryn in a discussion of "The Rule of Law," *Rev. Int. Dr. Comp.*, X (1958), 70–75, criticizes "ideal type" comparison and "transcendental values," and he proposes that comparative study be limited to what selected legal systems have in common. Except for a reference to the "presupposition" that these data belong to a common socio-economic structure, he does not discuss the basis for selection of the legal systems to be compared. He employs many values to define his "ideal type," including

fundamental rights of traditional liberties and their traditional guarantees. But he does not mention the functioning of the laws, "counterweights" to the specified liberties or various meanings of "independent judiciary." His thesis is that "what is essential is what is common." This might imply the vacuous generality of analytical jurisprudence (legal positivism) if no limiting cultural criteria were specified; it might imply criteria that are found in a primitive dictatorship which had the selected socio-economic structure; or it might imply common but unimportant criteria. What is wanted, however, are not only common traits but also culturally significant ones, actualized in a functioning legal order. Cf. C. J. Hamson, "La notion de légalité dans les pays occidentaux," *Rev. Int. Dr. Comp.*, X (1958), 5; Bodenheimer, "Reflections on the Rule of Law"; Hall, *General Principles of Criminal Law*, Ch. 2; Norman S. Marsh, "The Rule of Law as a Supra-National Concept," *Oxford Essays in Jurisprudence*, ed. A. G. Guest (1961), 223; and International Association of Legal Science. Colloquium Warsaw, 1958, *Le Concept de la Légalité dans les Pays Socialistes* (Warsaw, 1961).

50 Robert Redfield, *The Primitive World and Its Transformations* (Ithaca, N.Y., 1953). "I believe the probability is high that there are universal human values . . . ." A. L. Kroeber, "History of Anthropological Thought," *Current Anthropology* (Chicago, 1956), 301, stating also that his position is relativist. Cf. David Bidney, *Theoretical Anthropology* (New York, 1953).

51 With reference to the comparison of Western and Soviet contract law cf. Harold J. Berman, "The Comparison of Soviet and American Law," *Ind. L. Jour.*, XXXIV (1959), 568 and R. B. Schlesinger, "The Common Core of Legal Systems . . . ," *XXth Century Comparative and Conflicts Laws*, 68–69; and see W. J. Wagner, "The Interplay of Planned Economy and Traditional Contract Rules in Poland," *Am. Jour. Comp. L.*, XI (1962), 348. See, generally, David, *Traité*, 224, 319–22 and Arminjon, Nolde, and Wolff, *Traité*, I, 51–52.

52 M. Kareva, quoted by Harold Berman, *Justice in Russia* (Cambridge, Mass., 1950), 199.

53 *Ibid.*, 203–205.

54 René Dekkers, *Principes nouveaux de droit Soviétique* (Brussels, 1961), 12.

55 John N. Hazard, *The Soviet System of Government* (rev. ed., Chicago, 1960), 9, 11, 191–200. In an address to the American Foreign Law Association in New York on October 26, 1962, Professor Hazard, speaking about a recent visit to Russia, reported that in contrast to "Stalin's terror," there is now "a sense of what has been called 'the right of conversation' if not of soap box oratory on the public corner." He also referred to recent legislation imposing the capital penalty for speculation in commodities and currencies and to the retroactivity of this legislation.

Cf. D. G. Lavroff, *Les libertés publiques en Union Soviétique* (Paris,

1960) and W. W. Kulski, *The Soviet Regime* (Syracuse, N. Y., 1954)', Ch. 2. Professor Harold Berman adds that the death penalty has also been extended to "still other crimes, such as large scale bribery and resistance to a policeman . . . resulting in his death." *Harv. L. School Bull.*, XIV (1962), 4.

56 Dekkers, *Principes nouveaux de droit Soviétique*, 14.

57 F. H. Lawson (book review): "John N. Hazard, Law and Social Change in the U.S.S.R.," *Univ. Chicago L. Rev.*, XXI (1954), 783.

58 "A culture or a part thereof, Kroeber writes, must be studied in relation to the totality of known culture. By placing a particular complex against the grid of the known range of variation, its individuality or its genericness may be understood. The ultimate natural unit of study for ethnologists is the whole grid, all of culture. And we build up our knowledge of the parameters of culture by systematic comparisons, one particular culture with another, until we understand something of the nature and range of all of culture.

"These comparisons involve, the paper continues, three aspects of cultural phenomena, (1) content, (2) form or style, and (3) the values of the content and of the style. Content remains much the same wherever it is carried; form and values vary from culture to culture and from period to period." Mandelbaum, "The Study of Complex Civilizations," 205–206.

59 1900 Congress, 168.

60 Felix Cohen, "Transcendental Nonsense and the Functional Approach," *Col. L. Rev.*, XXXV (1935), 809–49, reprinted in Cohen, *The Legal Conscience* (New Haven, Conn., 1960), 48, 49, 33–76.

61 *Ibid.*, 466, 469.

62 "So far as I know the first systematic formulation of the concept as applying to the strictly scientific study of society was that of Emile Durkheim in 1895." Alfred Reginald Radcliffe-Brown, "On the Concept of Function in Social Science," *Am. Anthropologist*, XXXVII (1935), 394.

63 "Functionalists have explained their own beginnings as determined primarily by an attempt to get away from the evolutionary conception of social history and from the so-called evolutionary comparative method." Alexander Lesser, "Functionalism in Social Anthropology," *ibid.*, 388. "As soon as this term came to be applied to sociological analysis in anthropology, it was also used in sociology for the same purpose." Kingsley Davis, "The Myth of Functional Analysis as a Special Method in Sociology and Anthropology," *Am. Soc. Rev.*, XXIV (1959), 769.

64 Robert K. Merton, *Social Structure* (Glencoe, Ill., 1957), 61–66.

65 Radcliffe-Brown, *Structure and Function in Primitive Society* (London, 1952), 200; see Merton, *ibid.*

66 Ernest Nagel, "Problems of Concept and Theory Formation in the Social Sciences," *Science, Language, and Human Rights* (1952), 48–49; Nagel, *The Structure of Science*, 520–35.

67 "The Functionalists' persistent neglect of this historically demonstrated capacity for creating *structural alternatives*, and their often easy acceptance of what has been, or is, for what will be in the future . . . may perhaps be chalked up to the deficiency in historical perspective common to many of us in this country." Walter Buckley, "Communications—A Rejoinder to Functionalists Dr. Davis and Dr. Levy," *Am. Soc. Rev.*, XXIV (1959), 86.

68 Merton, *Social Structure*.

69 Davis, "The Myth of Functional Analysis . . . ," 757. Raymond Firth, "Function," *Current Anthropology*, 237–58.

70 Davis, *ibid.*, 771.

71 "Such 'functional questions,' when taken together, evoke a comparative science of society, because they are the most general that can be asked. The attempt to find systematic answers to them forms a framework of reasoning that can enlighten any specific inquiry, no matter how limited. Such questions, then, are not peripheral to sociological analysis, but central." *Ibid.*, 762.

72 P. 771. "Any science or scientific frame of analysis worthy of the name treats the interdependence of parts of a larger whole or system—including the major orientations in sociology." Buckley, "Communications—A Rejoinder to Functionalists Dr. Davis and Dr. Levy," 85.

73 "It is only in imagination that we can talk about a human group apart from norms . . . ." Davis, *Human Society*, 53. After quoting the preceding statement, a recent writer adds: "In large measure, however, small-group analysis has done its talking about groups apart from norms." R. T. Golembiewski, *The Small Group* (Chicago, 1962), 226.

74 Radcliffe-Brown, "On the Concept of Function in Social Science," 394.

75 Davis, "The Myth of Functional Analysis . . . ," 762–63.

76 Hall, *Living Law of Democratic Society*, Ch. 2.

77 Konrad Zweigert, "Zur Methode der Rechtsvergleichung," *Studium Generale*, XIII (Berlin, 1960), 193, 197, 199.

78 "Fruitful comparisons become possible when basic values are classified and the infinite variety of institutional detail is appraised in terms of its effects on such values." McDougal, "The Comparative Study of Law for Policy Purposes: Value Clarification as an Instrument of Democratic World Order," *Am. Jour. Comp. L.*, I (1952), 37–38. Cf. "Second, just as sociological statements or predictions are not rules of law, thus Professor McDougal's 'goal values' are not values, but only factual preferences of behavior." Josef L. Kunz, "The Changing Science of International Law," *Am. Jour. Intn'l Law*, LVI (1962), 496.

79 ". . . it is only democracy which confronts social problems, properly speaking." Frank H. Knight, "Science, Society, and the Modes of Law," *The State of the Social Sciences*, 12.

80 Bernard Schwartz, *French Administrative Law and the Common-Law World* (New York, 1954).

81 See Ch. N. Fragistas, "Les précédents judiciaries en Europe continentale," *Mélanges Maury*, II (Paris, 1960), 139.

82 See Lawson, *supra* n. 24, pp. 133–34.

6.

1 Hall, "Unification of Political and Legal Theory," *Pol. Sci. Quar.* LXIX (1954), 15, revised and reprinted in Hall, *Studies in Jurisprudence and Criminal Theory*, Ch. 4; and Arnold Brecht, *Political Theory*, 138 n, 329 n, 528, 555, 564–65. On the effect of the "structural-functional" approach in this regard, see J. W. Bennett and K. H. Wolff, "Toward Communication between Sociology and Anthropology," *Current Anthropology*, 329.

2 See *supra*, Ch. 5, n. 9.

3 For example, Lambert urged the study of political economy and he expressed regret for such concentration on legal texts, grammar, logic, and technique that "les réalités vivantes, les problèmes passionnants" are not seen. 1900 Congress, 56 ff.

4 Charles E. Merriam was "trained in public law." Merriam, *New Aspects of Politics* (Chicago, 1931), xiii.

5 In a survey of 220 anthropological comparative studies published in the United States in 1948–1954, only two were found in the field of law. Oscar Lewis, "Comparisons in Cultural Anthropology," *Readings in Cross-Cultural Methodology*, 62. The publications by Professors Paul Bohannan and E. A. Hoebel are exceptional. Even Robert Redfield, who was a lawyer, did little work in the anthropology of law. An excellent lecture by Professor Redfield on "Primitive Law" was not published.

6 See, for example, the UNESCO publication, *Contemporary Political Science* (Liége, Belgium, 1950).

7 Hyneman, *The Study of Politics—The Present State of American Political Science*, 23–24, 26–27. He supports this estimate in various ways, for example, in interpreting Professor David Easton's study of "authoritative allocation of values for a society" as meaning only a more intelligent and diligent study "of just what they (political scientists) have long been doing," that is, "the study of what legal governments do" (p. 141). Professor Hyneman also notes that research and doctoral dissertations "not closely related to legal governments are discouraged . . ." (p. 161).

8 *Ibid.*, 137.

9 *Ibid.*, 37–38.

10 Stuart S. Nagel, "Political Party Affiliation and Judges' Decisions," *Am. Pol. Sci. Rev.*, LV (1961), 843, and the citations there to other studies of that subject. See Glendon Schubert, "Behavioral Research in Public Law," *Am. Pol. Sci. Rev.* LVII (1963), 433.

11 Hyneman, *The Study of Politics*, 44–45.

12 David Easton, "Introduction: The Current Meaning of 'Behavioralism' in Political Science," *The Limits of Behavioralism in Political Science* (The Amer. Acad. Pol. and Soc. Sci., Philadelphia, 1962), 16.

13 Almond, "Comparative Political Systems," *Jour. of Pol.*, XVIII (1956), 394.

14 Gabriel A. Almond and James S. Coleman, (eds.), *The Politics of Developing Areas* (Princeton, N. J., 1960), 5, 6, 7.

15 See *supra* Ch. 3, n. 34; Ch. 4. n. 18; Ch. 5, nn. 9 and 11; and *infra* n. 16.

16 "Irrelevant, too, are the means of coercion. The friendly 'admonition' . . . constitutes coercion in our sense, provided it is regulated by some order and applied by a staff." Weber, *Law in Economy and Society*, 6. On p. 14, Weber notes that "today legal coercion by violence is the monopoly of the state." But the pages following that statement make it rather clear that Weber does not attach sociological significance to the State's "monopoly." For example, "we categorically deny that 'law' exists only where legal coercion is guaranteed by the political authority" (p. 17).

17 Hall, "Plato's Legal Philosophy," *Studies in Jurisprudence and Criminal Theory*, Ch. 3.

18 ". . . according to the Aristotelian view, the awareness of the principles of action shows itself primarily to a higher degree in public or authoritative speech, particularly in law and legislation, rather than in merely private speech." Leo Strauss, "An Epilogue," *Essays on the Scientific Study of Politics*, ed. H. J. Storing (New York, 1962), 310. "That right [to vote] is an essential ingredient of democratic 'behavior,' for it partly explains 'behavior' in democracies (for example, the prevention by force or fraud of certain people from voting)" (p. 312).

19 "Political power, then, I take to be a right of making laws, with penalties . . . ." Locke, *Second Treatise on Government* (London, 1764), Bk. II, Ch. 1, sec. 3.

   "Legal action—we may also call it 'political' . . . ." Ernest Barker, *Principles of Social and Political Theory* (Oxford, 1951), 45.

20 "How can culture, or at least Western culture, be imagined without laws? All of man's everyday activities, his government and his economy are regularized and given form by law." C. J. Friedrich, "Law and History," *Vanderbilt L. Rev.*, XIV (1961), 1037.

21 "Social life is possible for intelligent beings because of three facts. The first is law, a legal-moral-customary order sharply restricting the range of conduct to be expected; the second is collusion or preconcerting of activities involving mutuality. In free society 'the law' is ideally a generalized form of preconcerting; but, of course, much of it . . . 'just grows' . . . Third [is] . . . a large element of uncertainty and surprise." Frank H. Knight, "Science, Society, and the Modes of Law," *The State of the Social Sciences*, 16–17.

22 See Dorothy Emmet, "The Concept of Power," *Proc. Arist. Soc.* (N.S.),

LIV (1953–54), 1. Professor Emmet classifies "power" into five types: causal efficacy, creative energy, personal influence, ritual power, and legal power.

23 See McDougal, "The Comparative Study of Law for Policy Purposes . . . ," *Am. Jour. Comp. L.*, I (1952).

24 "A better approach, perhaps, is that of the lawyer, of allowing language and concepts to grow and be shaped piecemeal, in response to the emergent needs of a pluralistic subject matter." David G. Smith, "Political Science and Political Theory," *Am. Pol. Sci. Rev.*, LI (1957), 740.

25 An important beginning in the required directions has been recently made by Professor V. O. Key, Jr., in his *Public Opinion and American Democracy* (New York, 1961). He criticizes sociological studies on the ground that they "abstracted public opinion from its governmental setting. We have, consequently, research findings . . . whose relevance for the workings of the governmental system is not always apparent." His purpose was to study "how public-opinion bears on what government does" (p. vii). One may hope that recognition of the relevance of "what government does" will lead to study of law-as-conduct.

26 For a fuller discussion of this problem see Hall, *General Principles of Criminal Law*, Ch. 16.

27 Professor Talcott Parsons, whose contributions to sociological theory are widely known, reports that he has "never made any special study of the Law . . . ." When he discusses "what, from a sociologist's point of view, are the most important features of the Law as a cultural tradition and its place in the society," he is content to state that "Law, *of course*, consists in a body of norms or rules governing human conduct in social situations . . . ." *Essays in Sociological Theory*, 370, 372. (Italics added.)

28 "Science is built up of facts, as a house is built of stones; but an accumulation of facts is no more a science than a heap of stones is a house." H. Poincaré, *Science and Hypothesis* (London and New York, 1914), reprinted in Hall, *Readings in Jurisprudence*, 685.

29 "As yet there has not appeared a rationale that seems to guide political scientists in the selection of policies to be described." Hyneman, *The Study of Politics*, 39.

30 ". . . law has the longest and the most sophisticated tradition of thinking with respect to the embodiment of common values in practical social relations." Parsons, *Essays in Sociological Theory*, 165. See Thomas A. Cowan, "What Law Can Do for Social Science," *Law and Sociology*, ed. W. M. Evan (New York, 1962), 91.

31 ". . . there is a necessary connection between morality (how a man should live) and law . . . ." Strauss, "An Epilogue," *Essays on the Scientific Study of Politics*, 311.

32 Cf. Hall, "Law As Valuation," *Living Law of Democratic Society*, Ch. 2.

INDEX